ONCE HE WAS

The words and music of
TIM BUCKLEY

PAUL BARRERA

AGENDA

Agenda Ltd
Units 8/9 Kenyon's Trading Estate,
Weyhill Road, Andover, Hampshire, U.K., SP10 3NP

ONCE HE WAS The Tim Buckley Story
NO REPLY The Nick Drake Story

First Published May 1997

ISBN 1 899882 55 3

Cover designed by Michael Edwards using watercolour illustrations by Ken Brooks

CONTENTS

TIM BUCKLEY

NICK DRAKE

INTRODUCTION

To see a world in a grain of sand,
And heaven in a wild flower,
Hold infinity in the palm of your hand,
And eternity in a hour.

William Blake (1757-1827)

TIM BUCKLEY AND NICK DRAKE

When I was asked to write the story of Tim Buckley I was aware almost at once that there were certain parallels to be drawn between the career of Tim and that of Nick Drake. First and foremost both these singer songwriters had precocious talents, Nick Drake was born in 1948, Tim Buckley in 1947, so they were approaching the music business on opposites sides of the atlantic at the same time. Tim Buckley was first into the recording studio in 1966 at the age of 19, Nick followed in 1969 when 21. It is known that Nick was listening to Tim's second album 'Goodbye and Hello' recorded in 1967, re-listening now there are similarities in style. Very few songs from either singer were ever immediate enough to be hit singles but they both had their moments.

Their entrances into the music business proper were remarkably similar. Tim Buckley was observed performing by Jimmy Carl Black the drummer of Frank Zappa's Mothers of Invention. Jimmy Carl Black brought the singer to the attention of Jac Holzman the owner, manager, publisher, producer, jack of all trades at his own Elektra Records. Nick Drake was seen by Ashley Hutchins the bass player with The Fairport Convention, and brought to the attention of Joe Boyd, the owner, manager, publisher, producer, jack of all trades at Witchseason Records, Joe Boyd was also head of Elektra Records Europe. There was yet another connection Joe Boyd had leased his Incredible String Band to Jac Holzman at Elektra, rather than to his usual outlet with Chris Blackwell at Island Records.

A tape was made by Tim for Jac Holzman, and the exact sequence was performed by Nick Drake for Joe Boyd. Both Jac and Joe so enjoyed the tapes that they decided there and then to record first albums for these singers. Strangely later Joe Boyd started and sold yet another record label Hannibal to Rykodisc, he took a position as a director of Rykodisc and thus remained in control of Nick Drake's life work.

There is a similarity between the early albums of both Nick and Tim, with Happy Sad and Bryter Layter both have the same sensitivity, both albums are essential for any self respecting collector. Tim and Nick both became extremely poor in search of artistic integrity. Tim finally gave into commerciality after his Starsailor album did not sell, Nick never lived long enough to prostitute his art, he did however criticise many who had. Tim was a realist with a family to feed, Nick had doting parents who were always there for him in his time of need.

In Tim's songs the protagonists were for the most part people involved in his every day life, for Nick they seem to be more figments of his imagination. Do we really know who Betty, Jeremy, Jacomo, Mary Jane, Hazy Jane, or Joey are, or if they are intended to be anyone living or dead? There are also similarities between survivor Leonard Cohen's first three albums and those of Nick Drake. Cohen was full of deep poetry at the time and he was often mentioned as a sage of depression and deep moodiness. All three singer songwriters mentioned here wrote of their private thoughts, the investigations and learning what made them all tick adds to the beauty of their work. Danny Thompson the bass player played on both Nick Drake records and accompanied Tim Buckley at The Queen Elizabeth Hall Concert, which eventually emerged on record some years ago.

One wonders how many other singer songwriters would have been investigated throughout their work if they had died early. Would Kris Kristofferson had an alternative meaning for his 'Help me Make it Through the Night'. For example the song 'What's Another Year' which was the Eurovision Song Contest winner for Ireland some years ago has also been the subject of incorrect interpretation. The song is not for a lover who has left, it is a song for a man whose wife has just died, he sits wondering just what he will do without her. Listen to it again and hear what I mean.

So two extraordinary artists who both died young, both of over-doses of drugs. Nick in 1974 at the age of 26, Tim in 1975 at the age of 28. Their music will be with us forever, they will always be young in our minds whilst we grow old and decrepid. Neither Tim nor Nick left a suicide note, it is likely that they both died by accident, sadly we will never know for sure in the case of Nick Drake. Would Nick have eventually given in to easy listening music to get his message over is a question for which we will never have an answer, Tim did after takeing a couple years away from recording after Starsailor, but still never obtained that recognition except posthumously. We have their music forever, they can rest in peace in that knowledge.

Paul Barrera 1997

Without contraries is no progression.
Attraction and repulsion, reason and energy,
Love and Hate, are necessary to human existence.
William Blake (1757-1827)

7

IN THE BEGINNING

Anyone who remembers the sixties was probably not there
Robin Williams

Timothy Charles Buckley III was born in Washington DC on February 14th 1947, Valentine's day. His parents then moved to Amsterdam, New York, and Tim lived there until he was ten years old. The family then moved and set up home in Bell Gardens, and Anaheim in Southern California. Anaheim is close to Disneyland and is known for Oranges, hence the Orange County tag. Although not musicians his parents both had a love of music, Tim's mother liked the great crooners such as Frank Sinatra and Vic Damone, Tim's father preferred country music, his grandmother listened to Bessie Smith and Billie Holliday. Tim found himself exposed to a wide range of musical influences, he loved listening to banjo music, he marvelled the speed at which the instrument was strummed.

Tim's grandfather served in the First World War, he died in 1970 at the age of 76. Tim's father was Timothy Charles Buckley the II, the relationship between Tim and his father is more than a little vague. Tim's mother Elaine Doris Buckley (nee Scalia), seems to have exerted most control on Tim's upbringing. Elaine Buckley said that her husband was a perfect father until he fell from a ladder. This fall triggered a series of increasingly psychotic reactions. The marriage became extremely difficult and Tim's parents divorced in 1966.

Friends stated in interviews that Tim suffered physical and mental abuse from his father, but Tim has rarely referred to him in less than glowing terms. Tim often stated that his father was injured in the war whilst serving as a paratrooper, and this caused his subsequent mental problems, but this seems one of Tim's many romantic fabrications, it is not borne out by his mother's version of events. Tim also had a sister Kathleen, and his most enduring lifelong friends were Lee Underwood, Jim Fielder and Larry Beckett. Tim's father purchased a banjo and Tim started to take lessons, but later switched to guitar. Tim played American Football for the school team, in one collision he broke his left hand, the fingers healed crookedly. This meant that when he learned banjo and guitar he was unable to stretch a barre-chord. A barre-chord is produced by stretching the index finger across the guitar frets.
Larry Beckett and Jim Fielder were at Buona Vista High School with Tim, and from the age of 13 Jim and Tim played in school bands and other local groups. Another friend Dan Gordon was also a member of the early bands, he described these bands as unoriginal based on top folk/pop band 'The

Kingston Trio'. One group 'The Bohemians' featured Tim, Jim and Larry Beckett, then they became 'The Acoustic Harlequins'. 'The Harlequins' performed the Beat Poets type shows where one member (usually Larry Beckett) recited a poem while the other members of the band extemporised an accompaniment.

Tim then toured with Princess Ramona and the Cherokee Riders. Tim was just 15 and immediately loved playing to audiences, in an interview he said that he was playing lead guitar and wearing yellow sequined shirts plus moccasins and a turquoise hat. It was necessary that he became a school truant to play in the band. Ramona and her Cherokees played Oklahoma, Arkansas, Texas, and Arizona, Tim was caught by the school inspectors on a few occasions and sent home, only for him to return to the band shortly after. The school became so suspicious that he was checked regularly by the school inspectors even when he was off school for sickness. One of Tim's regular excuses was that his grandmother had died in New York, according to Tim she died many times that year. This was 1962 and Tim was already earning $60 per week enjoying himself. Princess Ramona was becoming quite popular in California but Tim decided that he would switch to playing solo performances singing folk songs at small local clubs.

At his last year at High School Tim met Mary Guibert. Tim was known as a rebel-rouser and Mary was entirely the opposite. Tim regularly made fun of her goody-two-shoes persona by bleating like a lamb whenever she passed him by. Tired of this incessant and degrading performance Mary decided to confront Tim. She stood up to him and asked him to stop, Tim immediately turned on his little boy lost routine and charmed his way into her arms. They became inseparable, and ultimately fell deeply in love with each other.

At the time there were numerous new artists appearing on the scene, but the folk boom and The Beatles were still to come. Tim met up with two other budding singer songwriters in Jackson Browne and Steve Noonan, they decided to start their own trio and they worked under the title of The Orange County Three. They never created the title themselves, it followed an article in Cheetah Magazine by Tom Nolan, he discussed the three musicians under the heading of The Orange County Three. They had been obtaining decent reviews in the local magazines but were totally unknown outside the Californian environment. Tim continued playing solo performances and some dates with the trio, he also got some excellent musicians to play back-up on some shows. He met up again with bassist Jim Fielder who had appeared with The Mothers of Invention and would soon be joining The Buffalo Springfield for a short while. (Later Jim Fielder would join Blood Sweat and Tears with Al Kooper).

Tim's mischievous sense of humour often got out of hand, it was once described as being similar to 'the fun' in Anthony Burgess' 'Clockwork Orange'. The Buckley entourage would often attend night club performances of local artists, as Tim and the others became more inebriated they would heckle the pianist singer, or folk singer. Tim acting more and more drunk would then fall on the floor feigning a feinting fit. Quite often the singer would become so tired of the endless heckling from these drunks he would say "If you think you can do any better than me then you had better come up here and show us". With this remark Tim would jump up from the floor almost totally sober, proceed to the stage and sing the poor unsuspecting artist off the stage.

Throughout his life Tim could never resist a dare and as you will learn later this sadly was probably to be his final downfall. Tim could sing many of Frank Sinatra's songs and his tour-de-force at the time was 'One for my Baby', his version was described as sublime, but so far no recording of Tim singing the song has ever been located. Tim had great difficulty in passing a Hotel fire alarm without pressing the button

At one of Tim's solo performances, The Mothers of Invention drummer Jimmy Carl Black heard Tim and suggested that the Mother's manager Herb Cohen might be interested in signing him. Herb Cohen was also manager of Lenny Bruce whose act was being closely watched by the L.A.Police, the C.I.A were also paying strict attention to the performances of another of Herb Cohen's bands The Mothers of Invention. Herb Cohen was also trying to manage Captain Beefheart and Larry Wild Man Fischer (both artists good friends of Frank Zappa the leader of The Mothers of Invention) and an up and coming female singer named Linda Ronstadt.

Herb Cohen was not the most well-liked person in the business, but Tim needed fathering and Herb was ideal, in fact Cohen's wife Janie also offered some mothering at times. Cohen and Tim Buckley met at The Trip a night club on Sunset strip. Tim sang a couple of songs and Herb Cohen agreed that he would manage him. The first gig was in New York at The Night Owl Cafe in July 1966. Tim was not an over-night success, there were many others solo singers playing guitar trying to make an impression to take over the crown already worn by folk sage Bob Dylan.

Herb Cohen approached Jac Holzman at Elektra Records to try to obtain a recording contract for Tim. Jac Holzman had formed Elektra Records whilst he was a college student, the label was fast becoming the most popular on the West Coast and ultimately went International with the butterfly label logo. Elektra were contracting and recording many new and untried singers and groups, Tom Paxton, Judy Collins, and Tom Rush were already there. Tim

10

made a demonstration tape of six of his songs and this was duly sent to Jac Holzman who was immediately impressed. Holzman decided that he wanted Buckley on his label, he could not stop playing Tim's tape he thought, in his words 'the songs were restorative, whenever I had a problem I played the Buckley tape'.

The Elektra album releases at the time all had that very special magic, their sampler double album 'The Garden of Earthly Delights' consists of tracks from, Bamboo, The Incredible String Band, Tom Paxton, Crabby Appleton, Roxy, Tim Buckley and many more, hardly a poor track to be found. The production was at the highest level and each artist's individuality was allowed to shine through. Tim Buckley signed for Elektra Records and started work on his eponymously titled first album, it was to be released in October 1966.

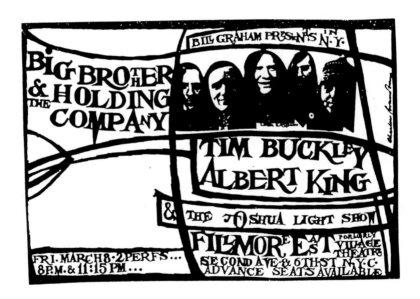

TIM BUCKLEY (Elektra EKS 74004, 1966)

'Time for the dream sequence'
A line from a Judy Garland film often quoted by Tim Buckley

Tim had more than twenty songs already written, and a small group of friends who were playing as his band. Lee Underwood was present on lead guitar, Jim Fielder on bass, Billy Mundi on drums, and Van Dyke Parks on keyboards. Tim and Parks had been staying in the same hotel, both were aspiring musicians and they agreed to appear on each other's albums. Van Dyke Parks finally got his chance with 'Song Cycle' an album which included a cast of thousands yet lasted barely 30 minutes. The orchestral arrangements on Tim Buckley's first album were from the pen of Jack Nitzsche, with production by Paul Rothchild and Jac Holzman. The studio chosen was Sunset Sound Studios Los Angeles, the resident engineer was Bruce Botnik.

Tim had always had a close friend in Larry Beckett they were met as school friends. Beckett wanted to be a writer and poet and Tim requested that he write some poetic lyrics to which he could add a melody. Many of the tracks on the album had been written some years earlier, on the album there were seven songs which were collaborations with Larry Beckett. The cover photograph by William S.Harvey of Tim leaning gainst a wall could have been cut directly from a mail-order clothes for sale catalogue. Tim is dressed in black polo necked jumper, white trousers and has black and white houndstooth jacket draped over his right shoulder.

The sleeve notes state 'Tim Buckley, an incredible thin wire, just nineteen years old, is already a kind of quintessence of nouvelle, the sensitivity apparent in the very fineness of his features. The man is a study in fragile contrasts, yet everything is in key, precise. His songs are exquisitely controlled, quiet, complex mosaics of powerful electric sound, they hold the magic of Japanese water colours. The voice crisp, full of strength and character, can soar, yet remain tender and delicate. This is Tim Buckley'. The writer of these notes remains anonymous, but to be fair apart from the eloquent hyperbole he (or she) is not far off target.

The album was recorded in three days, Tim referred to the cover photograph as presenting his 'Bambi' image. It is mooted that the letters LSD are barely visible at the creases of Tim's sportcoat but they are invisible to my eyes. The musicians on the album exactly perfected the romantic aspirations of Tim, the recorded sound is pristine. There is a marked similarity in Lee Underwood's playing and that of Robbie Krieger from the Doors, in fact on the slower songs especially we could be listening to The Doors. This was certainly because Jac Holzman was being ably assisted in the production chair by (soon to be) Doors producer Paul Rothchild. As Tim's album came first I suppose it is relevant to turn the influences on their head and say that Tim and Paul Rothchild influenced the Doors sound.

As a debut album it is brilliant, few artists have achieved the intimacy and quality so early in their career. Van Morrison's 'Astral Weeks' was not his first album but is one of the few albums that eclipses Tim's, yet Tim was much younger at the time of making this recording than Van Morrison was for 'Astral Weeks'

I CAN'T SEE YOU (Beckett/Buckley) is an up-tempo song accompanied by thrashing acoustic guitars. Lee Underwood carries the backing on a song of the sweet innocence of adolescence. The line 'Love is no sin, don't be ashamed' has been used many times to cheat women of their virginity, here Tim sounds honest and understanding.

WINGS (Buckley), a slow song, after the first verse we hear Jack Nitzsche's orchestra for the first time. A song for wife Mary Guibert, 'On wings of chance she flies'. A beautiful romantic love song my only complaint is that it is far too short.

SONG OF THE MAGICIAN (Beckett/Buckley), a song of poetic assonance. These are the easiest poems to write when the writer is equipped with a rhyming dictionary. The vowel sound is kept constant like smile, beguile, all the while. The melody is a shuffling waltz and has the atmosphere of a nursery rhyme.

STRANGE STREET AFFAIR UNDER BLUE (Beckett/Buckley), has the beat of 'Bend-it' a U.K. hit for Dave Dee Dozy Beaky Mick and Tich at the same time that this album was recorded. The song accelerates in the same manner of that other song.

VALENTINE MELODY (Beckett/Buckley), is a lovely ballad. The searching woman, she is angry and asking to be rescued. He broke through to her at Christmas, he cured her sadness before Easter, and the sun shone through her darkness before Valentines Day. Either Tim and Larry Beckett have got their chronology wrong or by natural progression it refers to the St Valentine's Day of the following year. I love the line 'The coin is in the air' indicating that they are taking a chance and it could go either way.

AREN'T YOU THE GIRL (Buckley) mentions a few times that 'It happens every time', and as this is the title of a later track on the album the listener can be excused for thinking that the track listing order is incorrect, but it isn't. The lyrics are a trifle arrogant as Tim asks the question of the song title because she now wants him. It seems that Tim is taking out his anger of unrequited love for another on a lady who is in love with him. He makes her ache inside just like other girls have done to him, inconsiderate oafishness. A song for the cruelty of adolescent love.

SONG SLOWLY SONG (Beckett/Buckley) includes 'waves washing the shore cymbal playing'. The song is gentle and calming with a polynesian influence perfected by the musicians. Long instrumental passages without any acoustic guitar from Tim. The song slows and stops completely half-way through and then restarts. More young love, she is sixteen and has beautiful hair, she kisses him whilst he lay dreaming, so the scene created was all a dream fantasy after all.

IT HAPPENS EVERY TIME (Buckley) sounds like a Byrds song. The track is very short, Jack Nitzsche's strings abound for a song of unrequited love. The sentiments are for a luckless lover, one day she will leave him, it happens every time. He is left tearful but still in love wondering why she can't be as true to him as he is to her. Knowing Tim's love life at the time this song is unlikely to be honest, apparently he wrote the song in the middle of the night whilst sitting on the bed of his latest love, Jane Goldstein. Her name was sometimes written as Jainie.

SONG FOR JAINIE (Buckley) is definitely for Jane Goldstein, a mid-tempo song for a street-wise woman who has loved, lost and learned. The lyrics state that Jainie has taught him how to love again.

GRIEF IN MY SOUL (Beckett/Buckley) is an up-tempo boogie blues. Again Tim and Larry have used assonance for their lyrics, here we are provided with ten thousand Heartbreak Heartaches, sorrows tomorrow, and a million woes though nobody knows. The lyrics are average but the band plays their socks off enjoying the rhythm. The protagonist of the song has a rainbow on his head, but due to his long lost love he has a reason to die. (To digress slightly on the Happy Sad cover Tim appears in one photograph to have a rainbow on his head.)

SHE IS (Beckett/Buckley) a song for a woman who is a bridge over troubled water, the bridge of love. In fact she is everything to him, the air he breathes, the day he walks through, the smile that keeps him warm. A song that is so twee that it could have been an embarrassment sung by someone else but it succeeds admirably. She is the bridge over the river on which he waits, appears awful in print but not when sung by Tim's beautiful voice.

UNDERSTAND YOUR MAN (Buckley) is a 12 bar blues rocker to complete the album. Similar to The Rolling Stones version of 'Its All Over Now', with Jim Fielder playing the strident bass in the style of Bill Wyman. Lee Underwood plays some great guitar licks, and Billy Mundi on drums is playing superbly. The sentiments however are a call from New York to California to his pregnant wife Mary. He is asking for her to understand him. As we learned later Tim was writing letters to Mary which were filled with his guilty feelings of leaving her for another whilst she was expecting son Jeffrey. A great rousing finish to a great first album by anyone's standards.

The album sold reasonably but did not set the world of retail on fire. Tim followed the release with a series of engagements in New York. He worked at 'The Balloon Farm' supporting The Mothers of Invention, and also at The Dom where Nico was appearing with Jackson Browne. Tim returned to California and played at The Troubadour, and then The Cafe Au Go-Go in Greenwich Village which had earlier launched the career of The Buffalo Springfield. The voice of Tim Buckley was described by Lillian Roxon in her Rock Encyclopedia as not singing 'blues modified rock 'n roll or raga rock as it had been described elsewhere', she said that 'There is no name yet for places he and his voice can go'. She goes on to write 'Tim's albums are the most beautiful in the new music, beautifully produced and arranged, always managing to be wildly passionate and pure at the same time'. It is difficult to explain the feeling presented on first hearing the album, it is even better than these words from Lillian Roxon, he really presented to an unsuspecting public a singing voice like no other, before or since.

The separations from his wife Mary meant that Tim was having relationships whilst away from home. Mary tired of being alone moved out of their apartment and went to live with Tim's manager Herb Cohen and his wife Janie. Mary then learned that she was pregnant and wrote to Tim informing him of his impending fatherhood. Tim was cohabiting with Jane Goldstein in New York. Mary then moved home once again to live with her parents for the final three months of her pregnancy. Tim was writing guilt ridden letters to her, full of cryptic references to the unborn child.

Tim was a regular party-goer and could often be seen drinking at The Dom with Jimi Hendrix, Jim Morrison, and Janis Joplin, a quartet of artists destined to die early. Tim saw Jim Morrison's 'Drunkenness as Entertainment' routine as adolescent, he referred to Jim as 'The baby'. Jim Morrison was to live nine months less than Tim but his posthumous success was destined be greater. It seems that during his travels he rarely spent time with his wife. He was living the life of a renegade maverick adventurer, which really meant womaniser. One month before the impending birth of Jeffrey Scott Buckley Tim and Mary met in a coffee bar and discussed their future. They decided

15

on divorce, Mary did not have an ounce of recrimination for him, she proved to be selfless, whilst Tim proved to be the opposite.

Tim was also presenting an extremely erudite image to interviewers, even though many times the references were cryptic. He said' It is a fallacy that torment makes music, we have white people trying to create negro soul music, yet B.B. King's diction makes him sound like a college professor, yet he still possesses negro soul'.

Tim appeared at 'The Bitter End' and his opening band for the evening were the up and coming duo 'Hall and Oates'. At 'The Garrick' in November 1967 and 'The Village' in Greenwich Village the show was observed by critic Robert Shelton. Shelton was revered, he was the first writer to really appreciate the work of Bob Dylan. In his article in The New York Times dated 14th November 1967 he wrote ' The concert was enlivened by a complex and frequently brilliant performance by Tim Buckley. He has the ability to stun listeners, he is individualistic and compelling, he is better live than on his studio recordings', high praise indeed.

GOODBYE AND HELLO (Elektra EKS 7318, 1967)

You can always tell a town by it's graffiti...

Tim Buckley

The production seat for this second album was filled by Jerry Yester (ex Lovin' Spoonful), whilst only Lee Underwood and Jim Fielder remained as musicians from the first album, the others had moved on to other ventures. Billy Mundi formed his band Rhinoceros which remained with Elektra, and Van Dyke Parks recorded his solo albums. To Tim's band Brian Hartzier and John Forsha were added on guitars, Eddie Hoh on drums, Don Randi on piano (he also played on Buffalo Springfield recordings), Dave Guard (formerly of The Kingston Trio) on Kalimba and tambourine, Carter C.C.Collins on congas (he was to appear on four of Tim's albums), and Jerry Yester augmenting on organ, piano and harmonium. Jac Holzman was again present as production supervisor.

The Guy Webster cover photograph shows Tim either wearing a monocle or perhaps a coin in his right eye, the 'Hello' of the title written in that 'coin' on the repeated photograph on the rear of the sleeve. Tim later informed Liza Minnelli that Pepsi Cola had asked him to use a soda bottle top as a monocle, if that is true then they could not have been too pleased, even with a magnifying glass the words 'Pepsi' cannot be read. This may have been another of Tim's regularly fabricated romanticisms. The sleeve notes this time are attributed to Larry Beckett whose collaboration continues with five of the songs included. The notes are in fact a Larry Beckett poem the last line of which states 'Crusading upward from dearth he will sing you his ten tales, and then wander till spring'. If the first letter of each poetry line is read down the page they read 'I Love Tracy'.

If the first album was good then this is majestic. More songs of courtly love, and packed full of painfully sincere references. Many of the tracks were allegedly written when Tim was residing at New York's Albert Hotel. This hotel has become legendary but not quite as important to music folklore as The Chelsea Hotel. The album does include some inspired orchestral arrangements but the orchestrator (even on re-releases) has never been credited. It was Joshua Rifkin he had received accolades for his work transposing and playing the piano works of Scott Joplin.

NO MAN CAN FIND THE WAR (Beckett/Buckley) can be many things to many interpreters. An anti-war song which has an introduction and a coda of an explosion. The mental war that is waged inside the minds of the befuddled leaders. A search for salvation though combat. The wordy moralising is undoubtedly sincere, soldiers prefer not to fight whilst the leaders send them into more battles. The nightmares of bleeding men, a bayonet and a jungle grin, orders fly like bullets stream. Graphic descriptions for a lyric that stands alone as an excellent poem.

CARNIVAL SONG (Buckley) a carousel calliope introduction for a slow waltz in 3/4 time. Possibly the thoughts and dreams of an LSD trip. The swirling of the melody as the images pass by, a song of instructions, learning by our mistakes.

PLEASANT STREET (Buckley) is a song for Tim Buckley to point the finger at the moralising of hippiedom. Stoned people in liquorice clothes, returning from the feelings of peace and love to stealing, wheeling and dealing. Whilst the hippie movement was gaining appreciation the genuine people were already being exploited by others pretending to be hippies. People were so easily changed to this new way of living, their naivety cost them so much, Tim's lyric is anti-freeloader and anti-drug culture. The hippies were destined to fall from grace eventually, Tim (and Frank Zappa) recognised the problem sooner than most, Zappa's song references on this subject were less subtle.

HALLUCINATIONS (Beckett/Buckley) has 12 guitar and orchestral strings playing in a manner to provide an ethnic Indian sitar sound. Roger McGuinn with his Byrds manufactured a similar sitar sound on his elctric 12 string Rickenbacker guitar. The vocal line also has tremolo adding to this ethnic ambience. This track could have been included on the early Incredible String Band albums it has the identical aura. Reverb and drug haze musical effects abound. The recipient of the sentiments of the song is unknown it may even be Larry Beckett's Tracy who was moving on at the time, it is unlikely to be Mary Guibert Tim's wife, she had not left Tim he had just abandoned her.

I NEVER ASKED TO BE A MOUNTAIN (Buckley) has Tim strumming his acoustic guitar through the introduction, Lee Underwood plectrum-picks his notes on his guitar in the left speaker channel. The group really play with some impact here. Mary Guibert does get a mention on this song, she is 'the flying pisces' explaining to Tim that she is carrying his unborn child. Who is the dancer that has Tim's affections, does she have the problems of the 'lies' from her former lover, or are these prevarications Tim's. It seems that later in the song he admits to the lies but then refers to Mary as his 'Flying fish'. Tim is exposing his heart to us in this lyric, he was feeling more guilt ridden than ever when he wrote the poem. The song is sung in a way that very few artists could ever hope to achieve. Tim seems to be ignoring the backing completely there is little connection with his vocal, however it all sounds perfect, off the beat and slightly out of key, so perhaps this is where Van Morrison got some of his inspiration for Astral Weeks.

ONCE I WAS (Buckley) is certainly influenced by Tim's favourite singer songwriter Fred Neil. The progressions of the song are similar to the last song on this album 'Morning Glory'. Tim is reminiscing for the love that has died with Mary after the termination of their relationship, people only remember the good times, he is wondering if she ever thinks of him. In the real world Mary was walking around Los Angeles six months pregnant so she had a constant reminder of Tim. The song is almost perfect, they had magic in their eyes, and silence in their words, this is sublime Buckley.

PHANTASMAGORIA IN TWO (Buckley), courtly love so far unreturned, he is so hopelessly in love with her he will do anything that she asks. He wants to share her pain, her sin, and he needs her most to take away his loneliness. This lovely song has the feel of a traditional folk song from where the melody is borrowed.

KNIGHT-ERRANT (Beckett/Buckley) is medieval love some of it sung in 'olde english', for example 'wither has my lady wandered'. The arrangement adds to the elizabethan atmosphere enhanced by the harpsichord of Don Randi. It is quite easy to imagine Tim singing this song in an effeminate manner just for amusement.

GOODBYE AND HELLO (Beckett/Buckley) This is brilliant it is two poems welded into one. Possibly the lyrics should be included for this song as Tim makes no effort to distinguish the double lines during the song. The lyric totals 600 words and the verses are taken in turn from one poem and then the other. This is clever an innovative if the listener can read as he listens, but meanings are obscured without the written text. The Joshua Rifkin arrangement is probably his best ever, it is hard to imagine it being improved. The rhymes of the even numbered verses are obfuscated by the second lines which commence 'I am young, I will live'. Cat Stevens performed the same style of song on his 'Tea for the Tillerman' album with 'Father and Son'. In Cat Stevens' song it is quite easy to discern which lines are for the father and which are for the son, not so on 'Goodbye and Hello'. At the end or each odd numbered verse Tim is saying goodbye to something, he waves goodbye to iron, speed, murder, ashes, and America, whilst he smiles hallo to the air, a rose, the rain, a girl, and finally hello to the World. It would be possible to wax lyrical over this song and the poetry for many pages, I just urge you to re-listen to a wonderful song possibly the best in the whole Tim Buckley canon.

MORNING GLORY (Beckett/Buckley) a classic in every sense of the word, Tim's most recorded song. It is melodic and accessible but pales into insignificance when compare to 'Goodbye and Hello'. Again the spectre of Fred Neil looms large over the song. Tim sings of his sense of abandonment from his 'Fleeting house of existence'. The last word of first line of Larry

19

Beckett's lyric has been cleverly moved to be first in the second stanza. The word 'window' did not fit the melody so it is moved. The comma after 'window' has to be ignored to maintain the tune which in itself is one of Tim's best. The hobo refuses to tell the stories and is then subjected to a cursing from the protagonist, and expelled from the house. What or who is this metaphorical hobo, is it death or perhaps just the spirit of Tim Buckley's guilt. Al Kooper took the song and added it to the first Blood Sweat and Tears album, it was this album where most of the listening public first heard the work of Tim Buckley and Harry Nilsson. Harry Nilsson later wrote 'Mourning Glory Story', a play on the name of this song, in hindsight a sad title for both Harry and Tim.

Goodbye and Hello is an album of immense sincerity filled with great songs that have stood the test of time admirably. With his impending fatherhood and a wife that was already abandoned Tim was writing better than ever. The album is such an improvement on the first, the team at Elektra knew that they had a spectacular album and the promotional team sprung into action. Tim always thought that this (and the first album) were songs of his adolescence and that after the completion of this the second album he had to grow up. The album also coincided with the fast growing flower power hippie movement in California. The love and peace brigade took the album to their hearts although Tim and Larry Beckett did not write any of the tracks with flower power in mind.

On 8th March 1968 Tim played on the bill of the opening night of Bill Graham's New York Fillmore East (formerly The Village Theatre). Tim shared the bill with Janis Joplin fronting Big Brother and the Holding Company, and Albert King, the stage was surrounded by The Joshua Light Show. Linda Eastman (later McCartney) was seen in the aisle taking photographs, it is alleged that Tim and Linda had a short but stormy relationship around this time. Tim was also linked with Hope Ruff, herself a singer songwriter she was known at the time for transposing the music for Sam the Sham and The Pharaohs.

Tim was working almost non-stop now as an headline act. He returned to The Cafe Au Go-Go and Troubadour. Tim made his first visit to U.K. appearing at The Middle Earth on 15th April 1968. He also appeared on the television show Late Night Line-up singing two songs. The song 'Morning Glory' was incorrectly introduced as 'Coming Home' this was strange because 'Once I Was' was the track used in the John Voight, Jane Fonda film 'Coming Home'. As mentioned earlier Tim's song 'Morning Glory' was included on the emerging group Blood Sweat and Tears first album 'Child is Father to the Man' which included friend Jim Fielder on bass. The song is sung excellently by the B.S.T. leader at the time Al Kooper.

Larry Beckett was drafted into the army and after Boot Camp he went Absent Without Leave, and served most of an unhappy year in Army mental hospital wards. Larry was subsequently discharged as unsuitable for military service. However Tim took the time that Larry was away to write his own lyrics for his forthcoming album 'Happy Sad'. Tim returned to Britain in October 1968 and Played at The Queen Elizabeth Hall as support to The Incredible String Band another group who were also contracted to Elektra. The performance at The Queen Elizabeth later became the Dream Letter Live album.

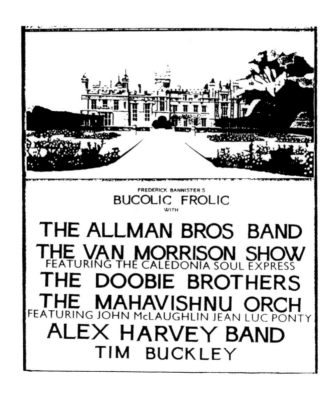

HAPPY SAD (ELEKTRA EKS 74045, 1969)

Sounds overflow the listener's brain,
So sweet that joy is almost pain.
Percy Bysshe Shelley (1792-1822)

Jerry Yester again performing the production but assisted this time by Zal Yanovsky from The Lovin' Spoonful with Jac Holzman providing production supervision. The ever present Lee Underwood and Carter C.C.Collins from the previous album remain, John Miller comes into the band on acoustic bass with David Friedman on vibraphone and marimba (later with Weather Report), there are no other drums. Bruce Botnick remains as the engineer although the album was recorded a Elektra Sound Recorders Studio, Los Angeles.

There are no hyperbole filled sleeve notes, the two Ed Caraeff photographs depict a thoughtful Tim Buckley. For the first time all the tracks are written by Tim, and the album is without doubt one of the most beautiful ever recorded. Tim has managed to create an ethnic music sound on many of the tracks, in interviews at the time he was declaring his interest in the music of Bali.

STRANGE FEELING (Buckley) a song concerning Jane Goldstein, she was setting up home with another man whilst Tim was on tour. Tim sings of love with plenty of sensuous moaning proclaiming that everything will be alright once this strange feeling subsides. The arrangement is straight-forward David Friedman on vibes creates the polynesian influenced aura. Friedman said that once he joined the band he changed it to be the MJQF, (The Modern Jazz Quartet of Folk). It does seem that Tim wanted his music to sound similar to The Arthur Lyman Group who had taken the charts by storm years earlier with their version of 'Taboo'. The arrangements on the album rarely use Carter Collins on congas, he can't be heard in the mix on this song.

BUZZIN' FLY (Buckley) a near perfect song, simple guitar introduction overlaid with vibes. A song that recalls an endless summer, it uses the basic theme of Miles Davis' 'All Blues' from 1957. Before making this album Tim and the group members sat for a day listening to recordings of Theolonious Monk, Miles Davis (Kind of Blue), Bill Evans (Nirvana and Intermodulation) and Gerry Mulligan (I Want to Live/soundtrack), to get into the necessary mood and groove. In the song Tim remembers the sun and the smile of a lady, she's the one he thinks about, she is the one he misses so much. All he wants to do now is walk hand in hand with her along the sandy beach, is it for Mary Guibert, Jane Goldstein or yet another new lady on the scene.

LOVE FROM ROOM 109 AT THE ISLANDER (ON PACIFIC COAST HIGHWAY) (Buckley) arranged originally for harp and vibes but no harp player could be found competent enough to play it in the style Tim wanted. Later Tim said that he would have liked to have re-recorded the track with Alice Coltrane but at the time he had never heard of her, he saw her later on the 'Today' show long after the album was released. Bruce Botnick the recording engineer made a mistake during the recording of the track, he has inadvertently switched all the dolby's to 'Off' and forgotten to switch them over as the recording commenced. In 1969 Dolby was not automatically introduced to recordings, it was a mistake that anyone could have made. The problem was immediately recognised when the track was played back over the system, the hiss was awful and distracting. Tim liked the version very much and asked if Botnick could think of a method of saving the recording. The result was a masterstroke, they hung two microphones from Tim's beach house on Pacific Coast highway and recorded the waves breaking on the shore. This was overdubbed during the quieter moments adding the extra ambience of sea and sand. If one listens carefully the hiss is prevalent when there is a break in the vocal, but as waves washing on the shore are expected it does not spoil the record in any way.

The song is one of the classic tracks of the age, John Miller's upright bass leads in and introduces the song with David Friedman's vibes. The song is beguiling and intimately personal, Lee Underwood's guitar sounding similar to that of jazz guitarist Barney Kessel. The lyrics state that her perfume lingers as he dreams of her and waits for her return. At one stage John Miller (his playing is outstanding throughout the album) adds bowed bass to Tim's 12 string guitaring. Tim continues his contemplations 'So it goes, my heart, your heart, our hearts together, all I know is let it grow and all you will find is peace of mind. Some of the lyrics are extracts from a letter sent by Tim to Manda Beckett (Larry's wife) but two questions arise. Why would Tim send such a personal letter to Manda, and why did he retain a copy of that letter to make a set of lyrics from it. The song is divine, Tim allows himself just enough space for exploration, the listener should be listening in the candle light with his favourite lady friend, sublime seduction music

DREAM LETTER (Buckley) is a madrigal well at least that is the nearest description. As a madrigal is usually amorous, satirical and (or) allegorical it seems that much of Tim's work could be given this title, but this track sounds like a madrigal. Tim had toyed with olde english on the previous album but not on this track. Lady time has flown away whilst he was thinking of yesterday. He calls for her to listen to his empty prayers, and sleep inside his dreams tonight. The underlying thoughts of the song is for his new son, Tim asks 'was he a soldier or is he a dreamer, is he mama's little man?' He continues 'Does he help you when he can?' The final request is the most heart searching and possibly guilt filled 'Oh does he ask about me?', a strange request expecting children to talk as soon as they are born. Tim obviously liked the song and he continued to sing it in concert for some years, I particularly like John Millers shuddering bowed bass that augments from the end of the first verse. The sadness and sincerity of the song becomes even more personal and beseeching towards the conclusion. Tim says that 'He has been fighting his own wars, how can I win them, I think about the old days when love was here to stay'. It is the final remarks that hit hardest again referring to his son he calls out 'Oh what I'd give to hold him!'. The listener on both this track and the previous has the feeling of voyeurism, we wonder should we be eavesdropping on such heart felt yearnings coupled with the over powering guilt of desertion and abandonment.

GYPSY WOMAN (Buckley) includes Carter Collins (at last) on congas accompanied by John Miller's bass, the more that one listens to the album the more one is aware of the amount that John Miller added to the overall ambience. Tim's voice is set a long way back in the engineering mix as he sings 'Cast a spell on me gypsy woman!'. The band is given free rein to create their own jazz-feel for this track. The longest track on the album at twelve minutes and sounds like an in-studio jam session filler track, it is just eight chords and a line or two of lyrics, the rest is improvisation. Lee Underwood gives an almost percussive guitar solo where he seemingly thumps the strings, David Friedman playing marimba adds the balinese ethnic sound. The lyric is extemporised around her gupsy spells, her mystery and her ability to tell lies. The jazz exchanges between marimba and bass are excellent, Tim introduces to us for the first time his desire for octave-surfing with his onomatopoeic moans, shrieks and wails. The song however presents soulful Buckley, he did have Curtis Mayfield and The Impressions 'Gypsy Woman' (1961) in mind when he constructed the song, however The Impressions' song is different. The song was used in concert to allow the expertise of the band to shine through, Tim vocalese became more manic as the years passed and in many performances this song would last twenty minutes, Tim never understood when the audience might have heard enough.

SING A SONG FOR YOU (Buckley) was said by Tim to have been written for Jane Goldstein. Written initially as a poem the lyric was created with considerable care and attention. One verse informs that the devil is dancing on Tim's world and is destroying his peace. He sings of starry skies all around, and of singing a song that he has known very long, please could she find the time?'. I have often wondered if Paul Simon used the idea of this song for his 'Song for the Asking' used to complete the Simon and Garfunkel 'Bridge Over troubled Water' album (1970), there are general similarities as both are singing a 'song of a song'.

The whole album although fully arranged sounds improvised. The recording was a labour of love for all concerned and it shows in the end result. It is alleged that David Friedman only played on a few tracks due to an altercation with Tim. It was reported that Tim felt that Friedman was attempting to exert his authority over the direction of the playing. With hindsight it is apparent that Friedman added so much to the tracks on which he played that this premise was unavoidable. To reiterate the earlier statement the employment of John Miller improved the sound so much, the lack of drums is hardly noticed. As an extra impetus for sales Elektra mounted a huge commercial billboard sign which had a portrait of Tim Buckley looking down on Sunset Strip. The 'Happy Sad' album remained in the lower reaches of the Billboard Magazines charts for almost three months, Tim was commercial at last and he was presenting to the masses challenging artistic excellence with little sop to commercialism.

Jerry Yester (who shared the production with Zal Yanovsky) was rarely present during the recordings he was away producing an album for Pat Boone with Ry Cooder, David Lindley and Clarence White. Whenever Yester arrived at the 'Happy Sad' recording he was jibed unmercifully for producing for Mr Clean, Pat Boone. The musicians would launch into a version of 'April Love' or 'Love Letters in the Sand'.

Larry Beckett had married his Manda after Tracy had moved on. Manda often said of Tim 'He was sweet gentle and romantic, women swooned over him, he had this power over people (particularly women), his concern over this power meant that he would ultimately reject his audiences'.

Tim appeared at The New York Philharmonic Hall in The Lincoln Centre, and one particular action during the show received massive publicity. As Tim was singing many adoring females were moving around the auditorium. Many items were thrown onto the stage as gifts, one lady walked to the stage and place a red carnation at Tim's feet. The newspapers stated that Tim picked up the carnation chewed it into small pieces and then spat them out. What they failed to add was that Tim said to the audience in fun 'Hey, that really tastes terrible'. The inference from The Press was that Tim was spitting back the devotion and love of his fans, when in reality he had just learned to his surprise that the taste was extremely bitter. Here was the first indication that the papers that had assisted in the creation of Tim Buckley were now ready to knock him down, it had happened before to other artists and it will certainly happen again. At this performance Tim also spoke occasionally to the audience, he completed the first half of the show with a version of The Parliaments' minor hit (1967) 'I Wanna Testify'. The Parliaments later became Parliament and all the other cloned George Clinton groups.

25

BLUE AFTERNOON (Straight Records STS 1060, 1969)

Music does not lie to the feelings
Franz Liszt (1811-1886)

Tim was particularly busy in the studio recording enough tracks for three albums. This album was used to tidy up tracks that were partly written for the earlier albums, he decided to purge his system clean of the old material so that he could then branch out. Jac Holzman was preparing to sell the successful Elektra Records label, Tim decided to make sure he had plenty of songs recorded and this album finally appeared on the Frank Zappa associated label Straight Records. Straight were releasing some essential albums at the time, Jeff Simmons released 'Lucille Has Messed My Mind Up', Jerry Yester and Judy Henske (his wife) the wonderful 'Farewell Aldebaran' and the crazy Wild Man Fischer his 'Evening With' double album.

For Blue Afternoon the band was augmented by the return of a drummer namely Jimmy Madison. The gatefold album sleeve included many photographs and some of the promotional albums also included a lyric sheet. The compact disc release in 1989 included the lyrics on the inside of the fly-sheet and the full album cover's four sides on the other. The music had stretched a little towards jazz since 'Happy Sad' especially the final track 'The Train'. The production was a solo effort by Tim Buckley, Dick Kunc who was Frank Zappa's engineer took over from Bruce Botnick. The overall mood and ambience is very similar to that of the previous album 'Happy Sad', it is all gentle and beautiful.

HAPPY TIME (Buckley), Tim in a happy mood dreaming of coming home to stay. This is another set of lyrics that could be a letter sent to his woman. The fears that she might sleep with someone else only appear in the final lines where Tim writes 'Let the morning sun warm your bed whilst I am away'. So whilst Tim was away fornicating he expected his own women to remain celibate until his return. A gentle song which one reviewer thought was a message from Tim informing the media that wealth could not buy his pride, if it says that somewhere then I missed it completely, love is the mainstay of this song.

CHASE THE BLUES AWAY (Buckley) straightforward melody and lightness prevail here. John Miller's bass leads the way into the song, he is in perfect accord with Tim's voice. The sentiments are for that moment when a woman finally trusts a man with her body, the instant when she floats away her woman's fear. The following morning she soars in love like and eagle. This is certainly one of Tim's most profound and beautiful songs, he shows the awareness of how a fickle philanderer wins the woman, the final two words are perfect when Tim concludes with 'For awhile !'. The sentiments are a return to those of the first track of the first album.

I MUST HAVE BEEN BLIND (Buckley) opens with the first few chords of Curtis Mayfield's 'People Get Ready' but that song was not to be released for two more years, so it was coincidence. This is song is for the occasion when one partner makes a mistake in love and then wishes that they could turn the clock back. David Friedman's presence on this track meant that it was probably recorded at the time of 'Happy Sad', his vibes are pristine and excellent.

THE RIVER (Buckley) great Jimmy Madison cymbal work and once again superb Friedman vibraphone. Rivers are becoming a recurring theme in Tim's writing alongside rain, mountains, bridges and home. Tim said in an interview that this track was not complete and that he intended to return to it later and finish it properly. He said that he would re-record it for a future album. To this listener it seems complete, and yet again it is David Friedman's vibes that catch the ear, perhaps Tim was correct in his assumption that Friedman was gradually taking over control of the group arrangements from Lee Underwood. The opinion that a man will change his ways if only she would love him is hackneyed, but it does not sound old fashioned on this song. Possibly a sequel to 'Room 109' and in my opinion 'In Time We'll Love' would have been a preferred title for this song. The guitars and cymbals echo the ripples of the river breaking against the river banks, although the identical sound has been used for waves breaking on the shore.

SO LONELY (Buckley) a song of loneliness, no letters, no visits, and therefore no ladies. A folk blues for being alone rather than a loner, which are two totally differing out-looks on life. The song may be two versions joined halfway through, Lee Underwood's guitar suddenly moves from one speaker to another, or alternatively the over-dub might have been set up incorrectly by Dick Kunc.

CAFE (Buckley) uses John Miller playing guitar rather than bass. He and Lee Underwood play from a stereo speaker each, as the bass also evident one of the instruments must have been an over-dub. (It may be that Tim is playing one electric guitar). The song tells of meeting a lady in the shadows, she is alone. She had sad eyes that sang when she smiled. His love grew ever deeper until she drew him near, and then once more love slipped away with time. This is the second song on the album that Tim said was incomplete, as both songs are almost perfect I would assume that this was another of Tim's impish rascally prevarications.

BLUE MELODY (BUCKLEY) sad and despondent yet one of my all-time favourites of Tim's career, probably because of the simplicity and the easiness of understanding, the listener for once does not have to work hard at comprehension. This song would have been suitable for Frank Sinatra, it has the best melody on the album. Lee Underwood now switching to play piano shows just how accomplished he is on this his second instrument. Lee's jazz piano plays whilst Carter Collins' congas provide a bossa nova rhythm, if ever Tim recorded a track that should have been released as a single then this is it, sadly it was never sold as a single, an opportunity missed.

THE TRAIN (Buckley) is represented by the guitar playing the chugging rhythm. Lee Underwood plays what must be his worst solo ever, it sounds like he is picking out a learning exercise which has absolutely no relevance to the song. I am sure he would be too embarrassed to listen to this now. The song which started with such promise degrades into pretentiousness, a mish-mash of unconnected tinkerings. The song relates of Tim being tired of New York and yearning to return home to the beaches of California, he wants to get some sunshine and feel the sand under his feet. Tim suddenly uses the opportunity to show us his gymnastic larynx with some shrieks and moans before the train rhythm finally returns and chugs to a stop.

The album just managed to climb into the bottom ten of the Billboard 200 halting at No 192. In an interview discussing the album Tim said that all the songs were written with Marlene Dietrich in mind, a statement taken with a pinch of salt. Dick Lawson in 'Friends Magazine' said 'Albums of such gentleness, beauty and profound sadness are impossible to write about, to put down in words, you go with it, or you don't, each cut is a hymn to a number of different shades and depths of Buckley mood', I just could not put it any better.

Tim wrote an article for The New York Times, an essay on Beethoven for The Beethoven Bi-Centennial celebrations, it was titled 'Even if you can't play him, on the guitar' by Tim Buckley Rock Star. Published on 22nd of November 1970, it continues with the theme of the title, Beethoven would have been the perfect pop star, but 'his entourage would have been a bit too expensive to take on the road'. Tim decides in the article that Beethoven is not relevant for the 70s, predominantly because 'you can't understand him'. Tim continues 'A classic of any kind is put away on the shelves, is always called a classic and is never read listened to or talked about at parties'. Tim thinks of culture like he thinks of bacteria, 'rock 'n roll keeps the traffic moving to an adolescent pulse'. Tim shows great insight and erudition, it is a wonder that he was not employed for more articles.

AN INTERLUDE, THE INFLUENCES.

The other arts persuade and influence us,
but music takes us by surprise.

Eduard Hanslick (1825-1904)

Tim Buckley openly admitted to many influences and many are detailed in this short interval. The serious music composers seem to all have used the voice as an instrument at some time. The jazz musicians were all special innovators and masters of improvisation. The writers predominantly came from the 'conscious writing' school.

(A) Federico Garcia-Lorca (1898-1936)
Acknowledged as a poet and dramatist he was not always as serious in his content as most critics lead us to believe. He certainly went very deep into his psyche for his poetry, I would guess that Tim Buckley particularly liked his work that was predominantly 'Stream of consciousness' writing.

Lorca was born in Fuente Vagueros, Granada, Spain in 1898. He was the son of a farmer and his mother was a teacher. It was mother who gave him his strong power with words, she also loved poetry so a loving son would always wish to impress his mother. Federico studied law and letters in Granada and Madrid, but changed direction to study philosophy. He had read all the spanish classics at a very young age. He was a student of Manuel De Falla who wrote ballet music and lighter orchestral pieces. Much of Manuel de Falla's work was influenced by spanish folk music and traditions.

Lorca's first publication in 1917 was a tribute to poet Jose Zorilla. Lorca was also a friend of Salvador Dali whose surrealistic paintings often invaded Lorca's writing. Lorca was also an excellent pianist and wrote lyrics for his own songs, some intended for use in his plays. He had a collection of poems published in 1927 called 'Canciones' followed by 'Romancero Gitano' in 1928. His 'Poema de Cante Jondo' was published in 1931. This work made Lorca the most famous spanish writer of his day. Between these publications he also wrote 'The Butterfly's Evil Spell' his first play, this was a comedy of insects, sadly it does not remain intact the final pages were lost and have never been recovered. Lorca wrote just twelve plays some romantic others highly dramatic.

Lorca went to New York in 1929 for one year, he also visited Cuba to broaden his outlook on life , but he became very homesick and returned to Spain. He wrote 'A Poet in New York' reminiscing his visit, this included an ode to Walt Whitman and another for Salvador Dali. His next play on return to Spain 'The Shoemaker's Prodigious Wife' (1930), although written earlier

29

and re-written many times later Lorca suggested that this work was influenced by Cervantes. Lorca also wrote a musical version which was staged in Argentina. 'The Billy Club Puppets' written in 1925 is in fact a farce thus decrying the seriousness considered to be prevalent in all Lorca's work. However it was the romantic and consciousness poetry that was to invade the lifestyle of, Tim Buckley, Phil Ochs, Leonard Cohen and other singer songwriters. We have to bear in mind that in English we are only reading translations and these can be difficult at times in the direction of accuracy of poetic meaning, however Lorca's work remains full of masterpieces. Lorca eschewed politics, he was most careful to abstain from any political rally or cause, his only cause was the world literature. When the Spanish Civil war broke out in 1936 Lorca was arrested tortured and then executed by the Falangist fascists as an intellectual democrat. 'The House of Bernard Alba' was published posthumously in 1945, it was the last of his Rural Tragedies, the earlier being 'Blood Wedding' (1933) and 'Yeoma' (1934). Lorca leaves a deep and wonderful literary legacy he was just 38 at the time of his premature death.

Tim Buckley used the surname 'Lorca' as a title for an album but it is difficult to locate an exact influence of Federico Garcia-Lorca in any of Tim's work.

(B) RAINER MARIA RILKE (1875-1926)
One of the most important poets of the 20th century. An Austrian poet born in Prague, he attempted to transcend the world of objectivity to create a closer personal reality. Rilke viewed life as an infinite existence, death is a continuation of life but on a higher plane. Rilke spent most of his life as a sad solitary introvert, he shied away from fame and acclaim and wandered the World. he was friends with the sculptor Rodin, (Rilke married a pupil of Rodin's), in Russia he became very close to Tolstoy whose work affected his own. Rilke's work is profoundly religious, the poetry has subtle rhythms, he was a consummate master of the language. His letters also became the object of admiration, long essays of conscious thought were published posthumously. In his 'Sonnets to Orpheus' the lines and speech patterns almost create a melody as they are read, it is here that Tim Buckley got his idea for long 'Letter songs of various thoughts'.

(C) JAMES JOYCE (1882-1941)
Irish novelist born and educated in Dublin by Jesuits. He was trained in theology and as a singer he travelled Europe finally settling in Paris. He became a teacher of languages and wrote in his spare time. 'The Dubliners' (1914) was a collection of 15 short stories all vivid clear sketches of life in Dublin. In 'The Sisters' we are provided with a boy's feelings for the death of a priest, in 'A Painful Case' Joyce reveals the story of a celibate man who refuses to fulfil his sexual love for a woman, and after her death finds that he

is alone. I am not sure if he would not have been alone if he had not been celibate, but perhaps they would have children. 'A Mother' is for an ambitious woman who ruins her daughter's life, and 'Eveline' is of a woman afraid to love.

1916 saw the publication of his first novel 'Portrait of the Artist as a Young Man'. This novel was considered sordid but presented to the reader Joyce's interest in mundane everyday life. Considered a landmark in the history of literature it created the new art form 'Stream of Consciousness' literature. The book details the spiritual growth of Stephen Dedalus through the fluctuations and nuances of his thoughts. Dedalus like Joyce struggles with his theological thoughts, he finds most things antagonistic from his childhood through poverty, ridicule and discipline. Finally he faces life accepting isolation for dedication to his art. 'Ulysses' was published in 1922 with the same basic feel as the previous book, but it was the style of writing that was special. In 'Ulysses' only 17 hours in the life of a number of Dublin citizens is covered. If 'Portrait' was considered a landmark then this book has been regarded as the most important and influential novel of the century. Set on June 16th 1904 in Dublin, the narrative follows Homer's 'Odyssey' ingeniously.

Stephen Dedalus is the lead character again (Telemachus) in search of his father with Leopold Bloom typical of the wanderer, as Ulysses. Dedalus in concerned over his conduct at his mother's death bed, and his father who is a un-salvageable drunkard is of little consequence. Bloom and Dedalus meet at a brothel where they encounter various fantasies, Dedalus incapably drunk is taken by Bloom to his house. Marion Tweedy Bloom his unfaithful wife concludes the novel with her unexpurgated musings as she lies in bed after midnight. There are many styles incorporated in the one novel, dialogue with stage directions, free associating, question and answer routines, parodies of English authors,(Shakespeare is compared to Dedalus' father whilst Bloom and Dedalus are at the Dublin Library), and even newspaper headlines. The book was banned in the U.S.A. and England for many years, but the work is hardly sensual or sexually erotic and is extremely tame in comparison with modern writings.

'Finnegan's Wake' was published in 1939 and Joyce's intricate language made the book extremely complicated and difficult, the crypticisms required hours of re-reading to understand the reasonings. The reviewers considered it an experiment that went wrong, it took Joyce 17 years to write. If 'Ulysses' dealt with the conscious then 'Finnegan's' is for the unconscious or perhaps the half-conscious. The protagonist Humphrey Chimpden has a dream which encounters the lack of love for his wife Maggie and his affection for his daughter Isobel and one of his twin sons Jerry. His incestuous and homosexual fantasies are paramount in creating the contention necessary in the reader's mind, to make this a work of puzzling but immense proportions. In the dream we are presented with fantasies, hidden desires, distant memories and sensations, allusions and myths, in many ways similar to 'Beautiful Losers'. In the dialogue Joyce becomes amongst others Jonathan Swift, Oliver Cromwell, and Adam. Joyce actually wrote articles providing clues to his hidden meanings of this book, W.Y. Tindall was quoted as observing 'as far as Joyce is concerned the pun is mightier than the word'.

(D) BOB DYLAN
born Robert Allen Zimmerman 24th May 1941. Recognised predominantly for his early songs and lyrics. Quoted by Allen Ginsberg as being the greatest poet of the 20th century, few scholars will argue after reading and hearing his early work prior to his motor-cycle accident. He did return to form later with the album 'Blood on the Tracks' in 1975 but it is chiefly his work before 1968 which derives most of the accolades. Bob Dylan has produced many more albums than most other singer songwriters, thus spreading his literate muse more thinly. Dylan also wrote 'Tarantula' in the 'stream of consciousness' style, of James Joyce and also has gained acceptance as a painter.

(E) ORNETTE COLEMAN, a kind and friendly man who turned the world of jazz on it's head. There exist legendary tales of threats on his life, angry people smashing up his instruments, and the members of a band just leaving him when he was playing on stage and never returning. His involvement with 'Free Jazz' created more enemies than friends. He admitted to his musical debt owed to Charlie Parker and was seen by many as furthering Parker's work. Coleman's work challenged many of the conventional laws of music, particularly harmony. Coleman scored a complete album for strings and called it harmolodic music (Skies of America). Started recording in 1958 on Alto Sax and soon moved to Atlantic Records. His landmark album 'Free Jazz' was released in 1960. He insisted on total improvisation, discarding old chord structures. In the mid-sixties his career slumped and he turned to various forms of music, but always in his own style of disharmony. Few artists have emerged who have continued his work, Pat Metheny is the exception, Coleman released a duet album with Metheny titled 'Song X' in 1986.

(F) JOHN COLTRANE. John Williams Coltrane was born in Hamlet, North Carolina in 1926, he died in New York in July 1967. Influenced by Johnny Hodges he arrived on the jazz scene in 1944. He was originally playing alto saxophone but changed to tenor sax after he had served in the armed forces in Hawaii. Worked with Charlie Parker in 1948, joined Dizzy Gillespie's band from 1949 to 1953. He joined the Johnny Hodges Orchestra from 1953 to 1955, and changed the world of jazz when he met Miles Davis in 1955. In 1957 Coltrane was in the Theoloniuos Monk Band, but rejoined forces with Miles Davis in 1958. Davis and Coltrane were too powerful for each other and

32

went in their own directions, Coltrane fronting a series of bands. His influence on jazz is massive, his albums are eternal. The album 'A Love Supreme' has been available since it was originally released and remains one of the greatest jazz albums ever.

(G) MILES DAVIS, born in Illinois in 1926, died 1991. Miles Davis is known as the father of modern jazz. Along with John Coltrane he achieved so much, by never remaining with one style for very long. His 'Bitches Brew' double album in 1970 crossed over onto the popular music charts. So many of Davis' band members have become famous in their own right, far too many to mention here. Miles worked with Charlie Parker, and then arranger Gil Evans, it was 1968 with the release of the album 'Miles in the Sky' that first made his work commercial. His film score for the film 'Jack Johnson' was exception but over looked, 'Silent Way', 'Porgy and Bess' 'Sketches of Spain' remain remarkable, his later work with rock musicians is less fulfilling, due to ill health many times Miles would just play a few notes and then leave the rest to the band. For his early more standard jazz try the Prestige Recordings, his later work was on CBS Sony. Tim Buckley claimed that he was often creating Miles Davis solos vocally.

(H) FRED NEIL, singer songwriter a particular favourite and friend to Tim Buckley. Tim sang Neil's 'The Dolphins' at almost every show. Originally from Greenwich Village he played in bands with John Sebastian and Felix Pappalardi, writing his own songs in the 1960s. He released some excellent albums 'Tear Down the Walls', 'A Little Bit of Rain', 'Other Side of This Life', 'Down to Earth', 'Remember the Future', 'Sessions', 'Bleeker and McDougal'. He shunned the publicity when his song 'Everybody's Talkin' sung by Harry Nilsson, was used for the film 'Midnight Cowboy'. The film also contains Neil's version of 'Cocaine' and 'The Dolphins'. The 'Other Side of His Life' was recorded by Jefferson Airplane and also Eric Burdon. Neil moved to Coconut Grove Florida where he assists whenever possible in dolphin research

(I) LUCIANO BERIO (born 1925 Italy) & CATHY BERBERIAN. Berio the composer and Berberian the opera singer are linked together for their influence on Tim Buckley, it was their work together that he had heard and attempted to use in concert. The two works of particular influence are on the same album, titled 'SINFONIA/VISAGE' and released on CBS Classics in 1969. Russell Unwin in the Melody Maker claimed that this was one of the most important modern classical albums of all time. It Was 'Visage that included Cathy Berberian she was already a talented opera singer her extreme voice range was necessary for the composition. 'Visage' was composed in Italy in 1961, and is subtitled 'A metaphor of vocal behaviour'. It is based on sound symbolism and vocal gestures, accompanied by their 'shadow of meanings'. This all sounds far too precious and is detailed on the sleeve notes, what the composition consists of is Berberian's voice accompanied by magnetic tape and electronic sounds. She (and the recording engineer watched by Berio) created voice sweeps similar to those achieved by Tim Buckley. This is not easy listening, it is extremely unusual and demanding. The 'Visage' composition was also used in the film 'La Prisionniere'.

SINFONIA composed in 1968 won the Montreux Award in 1969, it does not include Berberian's voice. Here the composer has conducted The New York Philharmonic, using the vocal prowess of The Swingle Singers. The work is subdivided into four parts, one part repeats the name of Martin Luther King. Text from Samuel Beckett's 'The Unnamable', plus some James Joyce coupled with student graffiti from the walls of the Sorbonne is included in part three. The work has the overall feel of Gustav Mahler, yet references of so many others such as Bach, Wagner, Berlioz, Ives are included. Claude Levi-Strauss the french anthropologist's book 'Le Cru et le Cuit' is used in the first part, they are part of the chapter on Brazilian myths. Berio's work is extremely demanding I would advise anyone who might investigate his work to first listen on head-phones.

(J) OLIVIER MESSIAEN (Born 1908) French composer organist, studied at Paris Conservatoire 1919-30, at the same time as Dukas and Dupre. He was an avid reader of Greek and Indian folk music. He also classified birds into region by their bird-song. He taught Boulez and Stockhausen they both continued with the idiosyncratic work of Messiaen. His work is influenced by Debussy's modal progression of chords. He also used exotic percussion instruments, and treated rhythm differently by applying unusual time sequences.

(K) KRZYSZTOF PENDERECKI (born 1933), Polish composer who won all three prizes in 1959 Autumn Festival. Taught at The Yale School of Music from 1975. An avant garde composer whose early work was influenced by Pierre Boulez. Penderecki uses extraneous noises as part of his compositions such as sawing wood, rustling paper, typewriters, knocking, hissing, shrieking and screaming. He also used instruments to make unusual noises. He particularly used the voice to add resonance to the sounds created. The singers were asked to articulate consonants rapidly. His 'St Lukes Passion' uses many of the mutated sounds and was welcomed by critics and public alike. Much of his work is based on Biblical tracts, he has written two operas, three string quartets, and many unusual orchestral works.

(L) IGOR STRAVINSKY, (born 1882 died 1971), Russian born became French citizen in 1934 and an american citizen in 1945. A pupil of Rimsky-Korsakov from 1903. Wrote his first symphony in 1905, followed by shorter orchestral pieces. Daighilev who had formed the Ballets Russes in Paris contacted Stravinsky and asked him to compose for his ballet company. 'The Firebird', was soon followed by 'Petrushka' and 'The Rite of Spring', the latter caused a riot. Stravinsky changed his musical direction every few years to avoid becoming stale, and he associated with Nijinsky, Picasso, Bakst, Cocteau, Dylan Thomas a veritable cornucopia of intellect. Not all his work was serious, he wrote (as his last work) his own musical version of Edward Lear's 'The Owl and the Pussycat'. The critics wrote of bare, soulless and expressionless music lacking in emotion. As his music has aged so well that previous premise is now considered laughable nonsense.

(M) ERIK SATIE (1866-1925), Composer and pianist, studied in Paris but was forced to play piano in Montmarte cabaret to live, he became a Rosicrucian and composed works for the sect. Satie composed just ten works in twelve years. His eccentric works gave him a cult following many young people were attracted by the humorous titles such as 'Three Pear Shaped Pieces'. He also used extraneous noises within his music, typewriters, sirens, whistles etc. He was instrumental in leading the listeners away from heavy Wagnerian works of the day to lighter more epigrammic style. His most ambitious work was 'Socrate', although much of his work was for solo piano. He also presented avant garde leanings in 'Grossiennes' composed in 1890, there are no bar lines and the score includes verbal instructions although these bore little relationship to the music that was playing. The U.S.A. rock bands of the late 1960s re-discovered Satie and his 'Trois Gymnopedies' was included as the Overture to The Blood Sweat and Tears eponymously titled second album. Satie had a motto 'Beware-behind the clown's mask is a serious composer'.

(N) YMA SUMAC was a south american influenced singer with a five octave voice range. She built her career around her ability to sing up through the octaves in her Aztec Love Call. Tim Buckley with his 4.5 octave range would not have competed with Sumac, she maintained the same resonance without resorting to the epiglottal at the top of the range.

(O) CARLOS FUENTES, mexican novelist. Has written plays and novellas many based on fact. His books are all written in Spanish with but have all been translated into English. Fuentes served as Mexico's ambassador to France from 1974 to 1977. He was also Professor of Latin American Studies at Harvard University between 1986 and 1987, working for President John F. Kennedy. His books reconstruct past and present histories, he sensitively explores cultural conflicts. Fuentes has won the foremost book prizes in both Spain and Mexico. Tim Buckley was reading Fuentes as part of his cultural ethnic studies. Fuentes had written 'Aura', 'The Good Conscience', 'A Change of Skin', and a book that might have influenced the 'Greeting from L.A. album title 'Where the Air is Clear'.

LORCA (Elektra EKS 74074, 1970)

Music, to a nice ear, is a hazardous amusement,
as long as attention to it is fatiguing.

William Cullen (1710-1790)

This album had been presented to Elektra before 'Blue Afternoon' but recorded later, 'Blue Afternoon' had included the musicians from 'Happy Sad'. This album completed Tim's contractual arrangement with Jac Holzman. The album was deemed years ahead of it's time when really it was just far too difficult a listen under any circumstances. Tim never said much about the album and Elektra released it on their mid-price range. The esotericism of the tracks probably meant that Elektra considered that it would be impossible to promote to the buyers adequately, it sold very few copies, and these mostly to hardened Buckleyophiles. It seemed so recalcitrant and iconoclastic and wayward in approach, almost so self indulgent that the listeners had to fight their way through the smoke-screen of meandering noise.

The band was Lee Underwood and Carter C.C. Collins, with new man John Balkin playing bass and adding occasional pipe organ. The cover shows a photo-conversion by J.Seeley to a photograph by Ed Caraeff, his picture on the back of the cover is another of a pensive looking Tim Buckley. The album consisted of five tracks the shortest at just under six minutes the longest at almost ten minutes.

LORCA (Buckley) a doomy menacing organ introduction, followed by a series of vocal acrobatics from Tim. The tune is just 5 chords repeated throughout to hold the framework of the song together. It is played in 5/4 time Lee Underwood again on piano. The backing represents an hallucinogenic haze gradually growing in intensity. 'Let the sun shine on your smile, let the wind hold your desire, let your woman's voice run through your veins'. Lee Underwood's piano sounds very similar to Joe Zawinul's who was a member of the Miles Davis group at the time. John Balkin on pipe organ holds down one note for a long time, Tim continues to sing in a different key to that played by Lee Underwood. 'Standing in the river, just stand and shiver' allows Tim to 'shiver' his voice at the coda. The song fades away after 10 minutes but probably went on for some considerable time after the fade. The title remains a mystery there is no correlation between Federico Garcia Lorca and the sentiments of the lyrics that I can discern.

ANONYMOUS PROPOSITION (Buckley) deathly slow, Tim singing in a deep resonant voice, frantic bass and guitar, free form avant-garde jazz, the song dispenses with rhythm entirely. This is another of Tim's letters or essays sung

36

meanderingly over the un-associated music. Love is just a slave to where the heart beats stronger. We assume that Tim is speaking of an older woman who taught him many things. He was just a boy from long ago, left forgotten, but lately you have wondered where he has gone. She has tasted the wine of men, who she has until they leave her to wake-up alone. Tim calls for her to love him even if one day she will eventually hate him. He needs to know how long she would care for him and where she would stay, the song then just fades away leaving all the questions unanswered. The song title should have been 'Slave to Where the Heart beats' it is the only recurring theme of the song, although to be honest, it is only a song in the loosest term of the word. Bafflingly pretentious the backing probably influenced by the late Albert Ayler or Ornette Coleman.

I HAD A TALK WITH MY WOMAN (Buckley) simple and melodious with lots of tasty guitar and at last some pleasant conga playing. The sentiments are a natural progression from the previous track. He is reassured by his woman that everything is alright, but he is not so sure. When she leaves his side he is like an half-man. Tim remarks that Moses and Jesus lost their way for some of their life, apparently they forgot their words at times. Tim intends to take her up a mountain to sing of his love for her, he calls for the sweet rain to wash down the streets for a little longer. Tim wants the world to be like it was before he was born. So this track is just a conversation with his woman, ideas come and go, reminiscences, thoughts, hopes, and for the listener it is little more than haughty and unconventional.

DRIFTIN (Buckley) drifts in, slowly and relaxingly. When there is wine in your belly and love rhythms on your tongue, sings Tim. Once more Tim is singing of an older woman who finds that every man is too young and inexperienced for her. It is apparent that she has been gentle with Tim whilst they were under the covers, he came there to hold and be held. This is a sensuous song of sex, the protagonist is dreaming of her when he thinks he has heard her bare feet on the stairs, but suddenly realises he is just a fool to his own imagination.

NOBODY WALKIN' (Buckley) up-tempo rocker, Lee Underwood picking out the beat and John Balkin playing one chord bass. Carter Collins plays congas in the right stereo channel, Tim's 12 string in the centre. The title of the song at least has some relevance, 'Nobody walkin', nobody talkin' nobody livin', nobody givin'' sings Tim. Lee Underwood also adds piano an instrument of which he is becoming very accomplished. A truly great song which gives the album the happy lift it needed, it was all becoming far too pretentious and isolated. Tim once more needs the rain to wash everything clean, he tells of how this woman has been 'turning tricks' up and down The Avenue, he has been watching out for her to see just what she is doing. By far the most accessible track on a most difficult album to invade, Tim has closed the door on our understanding, he wanted to bewilder and bemuse the listeners, sadly to the detriment of his art. 'Art can only be relevant if people are interested enough to pay attention', was a statement made at the time, not strictly true but the inference is appropriate in Tim's situation, he wanted people to listen, they ignored this album.

Lorca is not a satisfying album but it was Tim Buckley branching out in a new direction. The influences of Albert Ayler, Miles Davis, Ornette Coleman and John Coltrane were submitted as reasons for this change in direction, but finding those inspirations is almost impossible. Tim was now using provocation both in the lyrics and his voice to create a reaction in the listener. Previously he was soothing us to sleep now he wants us to wake up and understand. The album was released on the 'minority interest' Polydor Select Label and was made available as new product at mid-price (£1.9.10d / £1.48) and was deleted three months later.

It is much easier to play and listen to this album almost 30 years after it was recorded, but it is not a song album it is a listening experience and few people wish to take the time to investigate work which is deemed old and exacting, they sadly are the losers, the album includes some exhilarating passages and also some of Tim Buckley's most wretched thoughts.

STARSAILOR (Straight STS 1064, 1971)

Unfortunately, musical history is full to overflowing with unresolved dissonances.
Franz Liszt (1811-1886)

The fairest harmony springs from discord
Quintus Horatius Flaccus (Horace) (65-8 BC)

After the uncompromising Lorca this album was even more incomprehensible. Starsailor is an album that demands total concentration from the listener, but much of the album is bizarre and extremely eccentric. Tim had moved into a type of avant garde scat singing that was so powerful that one expects the singer to do himself serious epiglottal damage.

At this time Tim was at his physical and emotional peak, he had married Judy (Judy Fern Brejot) his fantasy woman and moved to a beautiful house on Laguna Beach. The rascal in Tim's nature came to the fore as he painted his house black just to annoy his neighbours, one black house amongst hundreds of houses painted white. The black sheep of the family. Judy was affectionately known as 'Madame Wu', the couple madly in love and totally intoxicated with each others affection spent all their available time together. Judy had a son, Taylor, from her previous marriage, Tim was at his happiest passing his time as a real family. The couple listened to the music of Penderecki, Satie and Messiaen before taking long walks along the beach. Their favourite music at the time was Olivier Messiaen's 'Quartet for the End of Time'.

Is the Starsailor album just difficult or is it innovative? Very few singer songwriters ever followed this course of onomatopoeic vocalising, but there again very few could achieve these vocal pyrotechnics. The band is the same as for Lorca except that Carter C.C. Collins has moved on to be replaced by Maury Baker on timpani and drums, Buzz (John) Gardner on trumpet and flugelhorn, and Bunk (Charles) Gardner on alto flute and tenor sax, both musicians came from Zappa's Mothers of Invention band.

Larry Beckett collaborated on some of the songs, during his time away from Tim, Larry had finally completed his 80 page epic poem for Paul Bunyan. Paul Bunyan was a 17th Century religious essayist and Larry decided it was time that Bunyan had a poem published as a tribute. Beckett failed to find a publisher for this work so it was fortunate that Tim had decided that once again he would like some assistance in creating lyrics.

39

COME HERE WOMAN (Buckley) opens with guitar runs and drum stick tapping, both the drums and the bass are forward in the engineering mix of the track which provides a sound not unlike that of label-mates The Magic Band, they were playing backing for Captain Beefheart at the time. Some of the lyrics are incoherent but the overall theme is that she is teasing him, enticing him but remaining just out of reach. He needs her and promises to be on the scene hoping to smell her perfume while they are drifting. If this sounds disjointed then wait until you listen to the track yourself, a strange track to select to open an album, anyone thinking of purchasing would be turned away after a few minutes.

I WOKE UP (Buckley/Beckett) is another dream sequence, apparently, and for the first and last time Tim and Larry Beckett wrote this lyric line by line together, they would normally write a complete lyric and then submit to each other their recommended alterations. The song is sung over extraneous musical noises, this is a return to the Beat Poets recitation over a musical improvisation perfected by Allen Ginsberg, Leonard Cohen (not a beat poet), Peter Orlofsky, William Burroughs and others. In this lyric the sun sets on the narrator's head as he wonders where she is walking in the wind, he flies above the shore over the town and the hills where he can hear the harbour bells ringing. A fortune teller relates how she can see his woman in the raw. There follows a Buzz Gardner trumpet solo where Tim has certainly told him to try and play like Miles Davis. The tale continues when the narrator wakes up, twelve sailor boys stand in a ring watching a shivering dancer rise out of the grass. Once more a lyric that is impregnable, and a band playing improvisation as an accompaniment.

MONTERY (Buckley/Beckett) this is the third track in succession that includes formless bass, the sound created is slightly similar to John McLaughlin's Mahavishnu Orchestra. A repeated riff and a few shrieks from Tim and a set of lyrics which may have been created by William Burroughs and Brion Gysin's 'cut-up' method of writing. The sentiments are supposed to be for a man separated from his lover. The poetic lines seem have no continuation, 'The vulgar (or Volga) cold sail surrounds you' 'I hurried away' 'holding inside a wheel' and 'lose control through the hollow' are called at us through some banshee wailing, Tim is also paying no attention to the rhythm nor the key signature, and remember dear reader this lyric is a collaboration !

MOULIN ROUGE (Buckley/Beckett) comparatively conventional when compared to the earlier tracks, a muted trumpet introduces Tim singing in 'tongues', well French first then English but never Swahili as Tim would infer. This is possibly for some Parisian 'Belle Dame'. An excellent song it is too, concerns dancing at The Moulin Rouge, the shame is that it is so short.

SONG TO THE SIREN (Buckley) similar to earlier work, this might well have been included on 'Happy Sad'. It was composed in 1967 and was used in one of The Monkees Television Shows (No 26), Monkee (former Elephant Boy) Micky Dolenz was a friend of Tim's. Tim had subsequently dropped the song from his live performances after Judy Henske had derided the line 'I am puzzled as the oyster'. For some unknown reason Tim was particularly susceptible to this jibing from Judy and changed the line. The melody on this version is different to that used on The Monkees' show. The siren is used here as a metaphor for all enticing women, the arrangement has a sound included to represent the siren calling. Sail to me, swim to me, let me enfold you in my arms, my foolish boat is trying to leave, on your rocks'.

This is a wonderful lyric and was inspirational for the group 'This Mortal Coil' which was a collection of artists that appeared on The British 4AD Label. The album was titled 'It'll End in Tears' and it was Elizabeth Fraser and Robin Guthrie from the group Cocteau Twins that performed the song. Fraser was known for singing in her own vocalese language, making noises rather than words, but altogether far more gentle and ethereal manner than Tim Buckley. Singing this lyric she wavers her voice like a sitar, the Song of the Siren really exists on the power of lyric, the melody line is not very strong. The version is wonderful and one wonders what The Cocteau Twins might have achieved with a full album of Tim Buckley songs.

JUNGLE FIRE (Buckley) is Tim wanting to be a Tarzan to a Jane or Jainie of course. The backing is formless extraneous noise until the rhythm section takes control at the half-way stage. All the instruments then play a riff in unison, extra ethereal voices are added Tim becomes increasingly incoherent. 'I heard your bated calls, you were there, you and I behind the sun'. Tim calls 'Mama Lion' which is echoed by the backing voices, as the musical riff continues unabated. Tim yodels through ascending octaves until the track just fades away. Tim would later say that this track was influenced by Eric Dolphy and Karlheinz Stockhausen, I would in argument ask, where? Tim was just creating the myth again, throwing influential names into the fray as an impish deviation.

STARSAILOR (Buckley/Beckett/Balkin) is certainly influenced by Luciano Berio's work with opera singer Cathy Berberian. 'Visage' had been written in 1961 by Berio and was subtitled 'A Metaphor for Vocal Behaviour'. It was composed for magnetic tape and voice, the version with Cathy Berberian was used as background music for Henri-George Clouzot's film 'The Female Prisoner' (La Prisonniere). The sounds in the backing are also similar to those used by Berio in his composition 'Sinfonia'. Tim includes stereo banshee noises and lamb bleats on this track. There is some considerable phasing on Tim's vocal recording as we get a few more 'Tarzan ape calls'. Tim also speaks in a very deep voice, the recording is created to make the lyrics difficult to discern, they are meant to be part of the overall sound, the voice as an instrument, singing in tongues. 'The wisdom of lips, wind, shape, suns, eyes, speak circuits' are all thrown in for good measure, the track misses the intended Berio influential target by miles. It later transpired that this track had been subjected to 16 vocal over-dubs after the initial completion, the listener will wonder if the original version might have been an improvement.

THE HEALING FESTIVAL (Buckley) in 10/4 time with an insistent rhythm, 'Black, tan, brown and white, nature, hope to turn the eyes and footsteps, learn for a while the healing festival condemns regards your constellation'. Well at least we get a competent saxophone solo in the style of John Coltrane to play the track to a conclusion.

DOWN BY THE BORDERLINE (Buckley) has a latin american beat, and a trumpet introduction. The guitar theme drives the track along until the drums take over. This is the track where the musicians prove they can really play. The lyrics have little co-relation except for the sun burning down on the borderline. A trumpet and guitar solo follow, 'Come on boy' Tim repeats and the album gradually fades away.

Tim considered this album to be his 'Magnum Opus', all the previous albums led directly to this. The 'Downbeat Magazine' gave the album a full five star rating. The album was slaughtered by the rest of musical press and ignored by the fans, the album was in the second hand album rack within weeks. There was another artist attempting to make albums in a similar vein. Annette Peacock released her album 'I'm the One' in 1972 which although difficult is far more accessible than Tim's 'Starsailor'. Annette also had problems keeping the audience's attention at her live shows, once she just let the top half of her dress fall down, suddenly she had their full attention.

The band went on tour and Tim took to barking and shrieking at the audience. Heckling became rife, and Tim was fighting an uphill battle not realising just how arrogant and pretentious his performances were becoming. He was playing just for himself, he was oblivious, ignoring the fact that his fans had paid to hear him sing and play, not scream bark and sing in gibberish.

After the release of the 'Starsailor' album Tim became virtually unemployable, his music was so dense and unique that it was not commercial. He also shed the image of the lost and gentle wandering minstrel in exchange for an aggressive and sexual persona. The record label did not need un-saleable product, if artists wish to express their own conception of music then they should fund it from their own pocket. The record labels have a responsibility to their share-holders and are not a registered charity. These points were put

to Tim who felt that his art was being compromised. The Los Angeles Free Press stated that 'too many of Tim's songs were now hardly worth the sore throat'. Tim could not obtain a contract and to fill his time he registered at U.C.L.A. to study ethnic-music, this was a programme of learning that was originally inaugurated by folk singer and folk music archivist Pete Seeger. The course studies the influences of polynesian music plus Japanese and Indian sounds and instruments. Tim often spoke of the Balinese Gamelan in interviews and said that he hoped to use the sounds on a future album.
Judy said some years later that she has no recollection of Tim ever enroling at U.C.L.A., but he may have given a lecture. Tim also took a job as a taxi driver, and later a position as chauffeur to Sly Stone. Again Judy says that these last two jobs were figments of Tim Buckley's imagination, he was continuing to create the myth, and fabricating stories. Judy said that Tim filled his time by becoming an insatiable reader catching up on all the classics, and also writing scripts with incidental music.

Another fact that Tim had regularly stated which was found to be untrue was his singing in tongues. He would tell interviewers that his vocalising was actually in Swahili, well it wasn't it just sounded like Swahili. Perhaps Tim was expecting criticism of his meandering vocal acrobatics and covered his ground by saying that he was singing in various languages, whatever the reason it definitely was not Swahili.

One thing that was certain was that Tim and Judy were running very short of money, Tim was drinking more and more and taking drugs. The road manager friend Barry The Bear Shultz did what he could to control the excesses, Tim and Barry became great friends in a difficult situation. Tim's behaviour was becoming more eccentric. On one particular show-night Barry Shultz was frantically trying to locate Tim. He was due on stage in 30 minutes but just could not be found. Tim was seen going into a launderette with a bag, when the bodyguards arrived at the Launderette they found Tim washing his clothes, sitting watching the spinning of the washing machine's drum.

Judy and Tim decided that they could no longer afford to live at Laguna Beach and the ultimately sold their dream house and moved to an apartment in Venice L.A. Lee Underwood quit playing guitar and piano for a living, he obtained a job as a journalist writing for Downbeat Magazine, (the only magazine that had earlier enthusiastically liked the 'Starsailor' album).

GREETINGS FROM L.A.
(Warner Brothers BS 46176, 1972)

It will be a great absurdity to use a sad harmony to a merry matter,
or a merry harmony to a sad, lamentable or tragical ditty.
                                        Thomas Morley (1557-1602)

Tim decided to take a break from recording, he judged that he was becoming stale and treading water. The truth was that he did not have a record label that would allow him free studio time to record his next album. The intention was to release a live album, but instead he took a holiday that would last for almost twelve months. He took time with his step son Taylor and his wife Judy.

He finally returned to the studio in June 1972, he had agreed to make an album that was accessible and commercial. Tim had dispensed with his meandering difficult music and now returned with a more melodious album. A new band was formed comprising Joe Falsia on guitar, Chuck Rainey on bass, and Ed Greene on drums. These were the mainstay of the backing tracks but the songs are augmented by many other musicians. For the first time Tim has used soul based backing singers and the team used by many others is included here. The singers are Venetta Fields, Lorna Maxine Willard and Clydie King, Tim said at the time that the album was influenced by the songs playing on the radio at the time.

An album full of energy which presents Tim as a singer enjoying himself and allowing the listener to enjoy the music once more, after the tribulations of the previous two albums. Recorded at Far Out Studios Hollywood with production by Jerry Goldstein (formerly a member of 'The Strangeloves'), who had also worked with the group 'War'.

The album cover shows a smog covered Los Angeles, the gatefold shows a postcard with a warning notice mentioning the atmosphere over L.A. and the temperature inversion problem. It is an original awareness greetings card by Mike Marcus and copyrighted by Pat Goggins. Tim is shown holding and wearing a gas mask. The postcard is addressed to manager Herb Cohen and Mo Ostin now executives at Straight/Warner Records. Some of the sexually explicit lyrics may have raised the eyebrows of a few people, Larry Beckett's poetry at the time was described by Tim Buckley as getting very close to pornography, this is nonsense the lyrics are risque, no more, no less.

MOVE WITH ME (Buckley/Goldstein) is straight ahead rocker with not much elaboration. The beat is insistent, 'I went to the Meat Rack Tavern' is the first line and sets the scene. Female backing singers for the first time echo the lyrics. At The Tavern he met a big healthy woman drinking alone, which he decides is a waste of sin. On my first hearing of the album I amusingly thought that he had said 'A waste of gin'. The suggestion is made that he could be her house boy, this would give them an excuse if her husband came home and caught them is carried through, however when he is caught and thrown down the stairs thus breaking his bones the epithet states that it was all worth while. Some of the lyrics are lost in the sound of the band, is Tim saying she is a 'black' woman surely not, but there again?! The band includes a Blood Sweat and Tears brass section, and a good saxophone solo. The listener might be forgiven for thinking that he has placed a Curtis Mayfield and The Impressions album on the turntable in error, a great start to the album and so unexpected the anticipation had been for a further stream of Starsailor ambiguity.

GET ON TOP (Buckley) is explicit, as the congas play the latin rock beat for a song not too dissimilar to Mayfield's 'Move on Up (1971)'. She walks across the floor to him, a slow burn walk, get on top of me woman let me see what you have learned? 'Let me talk to you in tongues' receives a whole new meaning in the manner that Tim sings the lyrics, 'Walls talking, ride with me' he calls, towards the end Tim decides to add some gobbledegook (good word for tongues, perhaps) for onomatopoeic purposes through the extended fade out. Tim is definitely singing in a manner more suited to Al Green and Curtis Mayfield, this is becoming Tim's soul album.

SWEET SURRENDER (Buckley) a track that includes cascading shimmering strings which maybe synthesized. This is a confession to an old flame. He wishes to explain just why he cheated on her, he had the desire to be a hunter again. He is back to teach her how to get a reputation, she has to prove to him what he could not prove to her. He was too hard to care, he was too hard to surrender to love. This is describing the mastery of sex and revelling in the ultimate conquest.

NIGHTHAWKIN' (Buckley/Beckett) is the track which Tim referred when he said that he had been working for some time as a taxi driver. Apparently the person in the back seat took out a knife and held it to Tim's throat. Tim (or the taxi driver) says that he should put the knife away because he was once a paratrooper. The fare was singing in the back seat being taken to 4th and Main Street. He only wanted to do the boogaloo whilst he was nighthawkin' for his change. The guitar backing from Joe Falsia is excellent, this is great track and might have served Tim well as a single.

45

DEVIL EYES (Buckley) is yet another rocker, albeit in a strange time signature, with a fast dextrous guitar solo and conga drums. This track received more attention than most of the others due to the lyrics, or one particular part of the lyrics. The narrator is tired of balmy breezes he is waiting for his lady to arrive, his 'Mama'. She has devil eyes that can see through him, she understands just what he needs. The electric organ solo heralds the lyrics that got so much attention as he says 'Get those black silk stockings down because I want to lick around those stretch marks and tongue between your toes'. Two fetishes for the price of one and possibly a third as he likes to perform 'the monkey rub' between the sheets, whatever that is. Tim once again returns to his 'singing in tongues' for the coda but so far there has been little pretension in the album.

HONG KONG BAR (Buckley/Falsia) written with his new guitarist, and probably it is Joe Falsia playing the guitar with Tim clapping the rhythm. Sitting in a Hong Kong bar dreaming of when he was 16 years old. Making love to an older woman on a freight train. remembering the seamier side of sexual achievement. Making love is like moonlight on the shore, yet it is apparent that all he is doing is dreaming, it is his fantasy. At least he paid her fare home, I wonder what he was doing with a pillow wrapped between his legs. This is Tim Buckley returning to folk-blues and an enchanting song is the result.

MAKE IT RIGHT (Buckley/Falsia/Goldstein/Beckett) is another soul rocker in the 'Impressions' style. He is searching for a street corner girl for a another 'trick'. He wants her to beat him, whip him and spank him, it will make it right when she is finished. Tim shrieks 'Make it right again !' followed by 'I wanna Beeeeeeeeee!' to complete a super album which startled the listeners into submission.

At least it was a return to music, the alienation of fans and critics to the previous albums was at last well in the past as this album received some excellent reviews. Tim was hurt by the criticism, that he was 'selling out' which was the majority opinion of the reviewers. The Press had pilloried Tim for his 'Starsailor' impenetrability, now they turned the knife by saying that he had compromised his art, could he do nothing right for these hacks. The pain he felt is understandable, he was unable to obtain work for his usual style, he had a wife and step son to support so he needed to work to feed them, and then he was accused of prostituting his art. Tim used an analogy in an attempt to explain his position, he said "The impressionist painters starved for twenty years for their art, as soon as one of them sold a painting for reasonable money they were accused of 'selling out', I now fully understand their position".

46

The mixed reviews were unfair but the music press journalists would be unaware of Tim's financial situation at the time, although I doubt that it would have made any difference to their opinions, impartiality has never been their strong point.

The album was as lyrically shocking as Starsailor was musically, the new love in Tim's life was Judy (she proved to be the love of his life), it meant that the Greetings from L.A. album was drenched in desire and lust. The lyrics do treat the eroticism with respect and affection, there is an absence of lying, and only a few admissions of emotional inadequacy.

K. BROOKS 97

47

SEFRONIA (Discreet K49201, 1974)

'Either the government slaughter you in vietnam,
or the hippies drown you in patchouli oil'

Tim Buckley (1947-1975)

Produced by Denny Randell this album again is full of new musicians. Lee Underwood returns for one track only (Dolphins) and the only other constant from the previous album is Joe Falsia on guitar. The nucleus of the group now comprises Bernie Mysior on bass, Buddy Helm on drums and Mark Tiernan on keyboards. This new group is tight and perfect for Tim's vocalising, and this is Tim's most accomplished album since Blue Afternoon.

The cover photograph by Ed Caraeff shows a saddened Tim, whilst the photograph on the rear is the opposite as Tim grins at the camera. The smile on the back of the cover is special, Tim with his arms spread out as if to say "As big as this" looks just for once as though he is happy. The cover design was by Cal Shenkel better known for his work for Frank Zappa. For the first time the album includes songs not written by Tim Buckley, and some of these were probably selected by manager Herb Cohen.

DOLPHINS (Fred Neil) at last Tim decided to record his favourite song by Fred Neil. Tim sings it well but the engineer might have improved the track if he had placed the drums a little farther into the mix. A song where the dolphins in the sea remind the narrator of the girl he lost and who may never think of him. Tim sings that this old world will never change, even the razor wire can't change it back again, as pertinent then as it is now. A song that will last forever, Fred Neil turned his back on fame and fortune when Harry Nilsson's version went gold when it was selected as the title song of the film 'Midnight Cowboy'.

HONEY MAN (Buckley/Beckett) the two writers together again, this time for rhythm and blues. He wants to be your honeyman, a euphemism for 'sugar daddy' one would assume. There is also The King Bee of blues fame, made into an international song by The Rolling Stones, whatever name is chosen they are all buzzing around her 'hive'. A superb song that was destined to be part of Tim's live shows for the foreseeable future.

BECAUSE OF YOU (Buckley) is another Curtis Mayfield influenced song. This is Tim professing his undying love and devotion to Judy his wife. Because of her he can face the world, she is the breeze he drifts upon. He admits to telling lies, and his blind love has allowed them to bring their dreams alive.

This is one of Tim's greatest love songs, everything jells perfectly the superb guitaring, the orchestral arrangement, this is sublime Buckley, a man in love.

PEANUT MAN (Freeman/Ludwig/Nehis) is a remake of Harry Nilsson's 'Coconut Song' (1972) which Harry sang on television dressed in a gorilla suit. Tim Buckley's first (and last) novelty song. Another track that would have made a good single release, Tim duets with himself via over-dubbing, the backing singers and percussion section are all enjoying themselves, the listener will have a silly grin on his face possibly because this song is totally unexpected and out of character from the usual over-serious Buckley.

MARTHA (Tom Waits) beautiful soulful ballad extracted from Tom Waits' own 'Closing Time' album, Tom Waits was also managed by Herb Cohen. It is an ideal choice and perfect for a Buckley vocal. Tim voice surfs over the melody with ease and precision, he could have released a wonderful album of saloon songs in the Sinatra manner. This is a song for a man who has been married for 20 years yet is still in love with the girl that got away. He calls her and asks if she would meet him for a coffee so that they can reminisce on the old days. There were no tomorrow sorrows, he says, they were packed away for a rainy day. This is so marvellous I still can't understand why it was never given more radio air-play, whoever selected the song for the album (Herb Cohen?) this is the perfect song for Tim Buckley.

QUICKSAND (Buckley) up-tempo song rocker concerning the pressures that can pull a person down. How deep does it go, sky closing in from above, there can be no paradise from flat champagne, yet once the party has started nobody can complain. Her sweet love is like a quicksand, I wonder how deep she can go, every time she touches him he is like a tiger. A special mention must go the Buddy helm's drumming on this track it drives the track along perfectly.

I KNOW I'D RECOGNISE YOUR FACE (Randell/L.J.Baron) is a question and answer song of which Dean Friedman would make a slightly similar song a big hit in 1978 with 'Lucky Stars'. The female part of Tim's duet is sung by Maria Waldorf. Most reviewers hated this track, I still think it is good and it sounds even better now, it has stood the test of time very well. The song was not written by Tim but the lyrics are particularly appropriate. She sings where can I find you, you have a son who has never seen you, he looks just like you. Tim sings that he is not carrying a gun, in real life it was reported that he was carrying a pistol for protection. The song is another perfect selection the sentiments that she has sent a letter many times that is returned with 'Not known here' upon it is a sad, it is certain that both participants know that they would recognise each other, and are still in love.

49

STONE IN LOVE (Buckley) a staccato rhythm for the certainty of love. As sure as the fox chases a rabbit, or the sun chases the moon, he is love with her. However Tim is saying 'I'm 'A' stone in love with you'. The song is a riff which is highlighted by a guitar solo in the left stereo channel, the lady backing singers add very little, perhaps this song was inspired by Johnny Mathis' song of a similar name written in 1972 by Thom Bell for The Stylistics. This track and the earlier Honeyman were the two tracks remaindered from the previous album.

SEFRONIA (a) (After Askopiades, After Kafka) (Buckley) is very strange, the lyric is just a list of unconnected phrases which never come together. 'Black coal burns (or turns) into a rose, she is lost in her own skin, is just a dream for a new dad (or Dada) in blue. The reason for the separation into two halves of this song was assumed at the time to offset the chance of litigation which had been served on Sly Stone for his silent 'Riot Going on Track'. Tim said in an interview that the song was only sub-divided to offset some strange english law, so it appears to have been true, he added that the full orchestra was over-dubbed later. According to the press hand-out at the time 'Sefronia' refers to a slave from Greek mythology, she does not appear in the song. The song and the title refers to an Ethiopian fable titled 'I have a cow in the sky but I can't drink the milk', so now you know. The cattle are mentioned in the second half of the song.

SEFRONIA (b) (The King's Chain) (Buckley) the join between the two parts of this song is perceptible, the sentiments of nihilism continue. I could buy you with a hundred cattle, I am tied to her by the King's chain, the chameleon lights in your dust-full eyes, the blue flies circle your head like stars. The last line is suddenly startling when Tim says 'I admit my weakness for your dark nipples'. A song in the Starsailor mould which Tim has slipped into the album to maintain his own musical direction, at least for one track. Sadly it fails miserably, the listener tires trying to hear a complete line of lyrics, some of the words are deliberately obfuscated.

SALLY GO ROUND THE ROSES (Traditional arr Buckley) sung with Tim's own lyrics. Originally a hit for The Jaynetts a female group from The Bronx, composed that time by Zelma Sanders in 1963, that version reached No 2 in the Billboard charts. Tim's version created some interest due to the fact that Tim was singing of a girl who had left her man for the love of another woman. To drown his sorrows he was intending to go out dancing and drink himself blind. He was revelling in his new found freedom, listening to that juke box melody. Taken at a steady beat with the bass player deciding that playing one note throughout was sufficient.

50

A great album which deserved more success but Tim had almost lost his fan following. This was an album of compromise after the mediocre reception of The Greetings from L.A. album. The Sefronia song seemingly almost surreptitiously sneaked onto the album.

Tim said in an interview that Sefronia was his favourite album, but many artists say that of their latest release. Tim visited Britain and performed at The Knebworth Festival in July 1974, but for some reason the organisers placed him first on the bill, a position usually reserved for supporting artists. Tim brought his own band across from the states and friend and old time associate Jim Fielder was included on bass, new drinking partner Art Johnson was on guitar. Tim gave a magnificent performance singing amongst others 'Dolphins' and 'Buzzin' Fly'. The artists that followed Tim on the bill at Knebworth were Alex Harvey, The Doobie Brothers, Van Morrison, and The Allman Brothers Band.

As mentioned earlier, there had been some criticism, mostly by his doting fans, that Tim had been selected to open the show as the support act, but he was certainly the least commercially popular of the acts appearing that day. Tim told Andy Childs at Zig Zag magazine after this album that "There are fewer things in my life than I want to do now, but I want to live them more intensely". After the appearance at Knebworth Tim returned to New York and opened a show in New York's Central Park. Jim Fielder was present on bass, and it was Jim's former band Blood Sweat and Tears that were the headliners of the show. Tim and his group played for 75 minutes and received a great reception for the performance.

LOOK AT THE FOOL (Discreet K 59204, 1974)

'Singers never die they just go to Las Vegas'
Tim Buckley (1947-1975)

The anticipation for this album after the joys of Sefronia and Tim's Knebworth Festival appearance were not to be realised. Apparently this album's title was changed at the last minute. Originally titled 'Another American Souvenir'. It is the quality of the songs that spoils the album. Tim is singing as well as ever and putting his heart and soul into the recordings but there is little innovation on show in this release.

Joe Falsia has taken over the production and had also arranged the songs. Recorded at Wally Heider's studio, Heider has personally performed the overdubbing. The cover design for the first time is a painting by Napoleon, but his surname is not provided. The photographs by Norman Seeff are of a sad and miserable Tim Buckley somewhat similar to the cover of Sefronia. The line-up of the band is different on each track, Jim Fielder and Chuck Rainey both play bass on a couple of the songs, with Jim Hughes playing bass on the others. Joe Falsia is the only constant alongside Tim, the record includes a brass section and a trio of female backing singers.

LOOK AT THE FOOL (Buckley) is a nice mid-tempo song, the title should really be 'Look at the fool, that made me cry', the fool being Tim himself. In the lyrics Tim states ' I love you more than I love my self even though you are doing things to my health'. This is not a love song to a woman as most of the reviewers thought, he is singing of his dependence on Jack Daniels alcohol. He can't live without it, it is wrong but he can't do without it. Through the song the listener is aware that there has been a slight change in the timbre of Tim's voice. He now sounds like Boz Scaggs the singer guitarist from The Steve Miller Band. Scaggs had gone solo and was releasing albums filled with songs like this opening track of Tim's album. Scaggs wrote and sang 'We're All Alone' a hit for Rita Coolidge and others but not for Boz himself.

BRING IT ON UP (Buckley) has some great drumming from Earl Palmer, and includes a line sometimes used by Tim for special effect in live shows, 'Belly to belly darling'. The problem with this track is the engineering, the backing singers are mixed louder than Tim and many of his lyrics are lost. It is apparent that Tim can't carry the load alone, he tells his lady to throw away those pills so that they can have some good time living, they are going to turn the tide around. An average song in the Marvin Gaye and Curtis Mayfield style.

HELPLESS (Buckley), is a call for a woman to come and love him until he is helpless. Again there is the inference that alcohol is the love in question. Love like a skinned red cat crawling across the highway, he sings, he adds, you bring my sex alive. Alcohol heightens the desire but reduces the performance, the song would have been an ideal single release. King Errison is playing congas and sounds exactly the same as Carter C.C.Collins, perhaps a little more calypso in the bongo taps from Errison. The tune harks back to 'Peanut Man' on the previous album, which in turn was very similar to 'Coconut' from Harry Nilsson's 'Nilsson Schmilsson' album.

FREEWAY BLUES (Buckley/Beckett) is different in sound due to the extra echo (reverb) added to Tim's vocal. He is singing in his bluesy nasal voice too, at the end of each verse the writers have added their list of 'blues' with each list ending with 'Rocket ship blues'. As Elton John's record label was Rocket Records perhaps Tim's strange vocal is his impression of Elton. A great fun song of a man who wants to throw a party but has the fear that nobody will arrive, the situartion is for drinkers have a phobia of not drinking alone. There are very few amusing songs in the Tim Buckley (and Larry Beckett) canon, and they are a surprise when they are included, however this one has serious under-tones.

TIJUANA MOON (Buckley/Beckett) commences with the line 'the padre told me all the hymns were born out of a saxophone', a strange assumption. This song has the sound of some of Frank Zappa's arrangements, a decent riff in search of a melody. A festival beneath the Tijuana moon, he dreams of a tijuana moon, the brass section is set deep into the mix. A strange song which says very little, and it took two writers to compose.

AIN'T IT PECULIAR (Buckley) has a duration of 214 minutes and not 154 as detailed on the track listing. The title leads the listener to anticipate that this might be a version of Marvin Gaye's 'Aint that Peculiar' but it would be an incorrect assumption. This is a list of un-connected musings, he misses her smile, he is the talk of the town, when will the long night ever end, next minute busted and listening to the prison sound, double talk is the rule of the game, the back-stabbing practice drives you insane. The last of these may be Tim directing his bile towards the music press who seem to be unsatisfied with whatever Tim attempts.

WHO COULD DENY YOU (Buckley) is a song that reminds the listener of 'The Big Hurt' a song that was a massive hit in 1959 for Miss Toni Fisher in the U.S.A., and later recorded by other artists, the definitive version by The late Del Shannon. Mike Melvion adds synthesizer to this superb soul song. A song for a man consoling a woman, he knows her kind, she has been through the mill, she is crying over the one that got away, her first love. She ended up with someone else on the rebound, the sentiments are a repeat of the Tom Waits' song Martha on the 'Sefronia' album. Please don't tease me I am here lying beside you, implores the man, but of course her thoughts are for another. The song has a change of rhythm towards the ending, it allows Tim to repeat the title ad finitem in the style of James Brown.

MEXICALI VOODOO (Buckley) the midnight train from Yuma travels down to Mexicali, he wants to visit Madame Wu's. The song should have been longer it never really gets going, what we have here is no more than a meandering ramble. Madame Wu's is some special establishment, three days later you wake up in an elevator ready to meet your maker. Tim takes some of the voice trills used in hispanic folk song, perhaps he was remembering Richie Valens' La Bamba when he was recording the song.

DOWN IN THE STREET (Buckley) has Tim singing more of his musings, he seems bemused and the disjointed thoughts again have no solution. High rise gang control, a particularly interesting thought is that in the U.S.A. there is a great deal of room at the top but nowhere to sit down. The summer is coming it will bring tornados, a rock 'n roll Jesus, guns shots in the night, but relax tonight it is not your turn to be killed. As the City moans under the increasing pressures the backing singers coda the song by repeating the word 'Summertime' until the fade-out arrives.

WANDA LOU (Buckley) is the Kingsmen's 'Louie Louie' revisited, well the tune is. If one listens to the original 'Louie Louie' then only the title can be discerned correctly, the rest of the lyrics are obfuscated in mumbling, not so on Tim's version. A special mention is necessary for the drumming of ex-Taj Mahal (and B.B.King) drummer Earl Palmer who plays brilliantly throughout the album. Wanda Lou can you ever be true, Wanda Lu is Tim's affectionate term for his wife Judy, and sadly it was to be the last song of Tim's career, quite fitting that it should be directed at Judy the love of his life.

Tim was still unhappy with the music he was recording, compromising his art. He told his mother this fact but of course she would have been happier with Tim singing in his best crooning Frank Sinatra voice. The music is far from his Starsailor period, his fans had deserted him then but sadly this album would not bring them back. There are so many influences on show, Boz Scaggs, Elton John, Marvin Gaye, Curtis Mayfield, Al Green, Frank Zappa and even James Brown, there is very little of the old style Tim Buckley of the first four albums.

Tim attended a reception to meet the Press and discuss this latest album. Tim was late in arriving and once he was there he was in discussions and signing autographs. Old friend Joe Stevens arrived and as soon as Tim saw him he jumped up embraced Joe and said "Hi Joe, let's get out of here", and they went, leaving his manager and the executives of Discreet astounded and furious. Tim remained at Joe's house for two days watching television and drinking. Joe Stevens remembers that his impression of Tim at the time was that he had become old and was constantly frowning, he rarely smiled any more. Joe Stevens was also accused of 'kidnapping' Tim from the press reception an allegation he refutes, it was Tim's idea to leave not his, Joe had no idea how long the reception had been in progress when he had arrived.

K BROOKS 97

THE END

The talented ones are the careless ones,
those with too little time.

The late Malcolm Lowry

In this final year Tim lived in what could be termed controlled schizophrenia. This description came from friend Lee Underwood. Tim had been providing just what the record labels needed so that he could at least be recorded and earn some money. He was learning to live with this dilemma, and often spoke of returning to country and western music. Tim drank heavily usually Jack Daniels Black, and ate rarely. Towards the end of Tim's drinking session his mind would turn to sex and attempts to find a suitable lady were undertaken. Tim was also carrying a pistol, he was fearful that he might be attacked. There were many local objectors who resented people with long hair, Tim's view was that if you were attacked when you were carrying a gun then at least you stood a chance.

One of his last projects was that he was working with Larry Beckett on a script adapted from Joseph Conrad's novel 'Out of the Islands'. It is thought that the out-come of this work would have been a thematic album. Tim also was working on a recording project which would retrospect his complete career. The idea was for a chronological live album with selected songs from his albums each played with the original musicians. It is mooted that Tim actually started to collect material and contact musicians for this project in April 1975, he was intending to record the double album on stage without an audience over a two week period. The idea was well discussed he told Zig Zag magazine in an interview in April that 'Goodbye and Hello' would not be included as it needed a full orchestra to sound authentic. Another project was started but remained unfinished, Tim was also scripting Thomas Wolfe's 'You Can't Go Home Again', but on this script he seems to have worked alone.

Throughout his career Tim often referred to a script he had written titled 'Air Conditioned Inside', Tim said it was a sort of 'Fear and Loathing in Dallas', and had Buckminster Fuller influences. He said that it was complete both the dialogue and the incidental music, yet none of it has ever been found. Tim spent some time searching for capital to make the film or show, but as this was after the infamous Starsailor album he could not find a backer. The plot is of a musician who blows up an audience that consistently asks for songs from the earlier section of his career. The story has many dream sequences based on fantasy, the musician eventually makes his escape tucked under the wings of a vulture. The surrealistic finish of this phoenix-like flight is exacerbated by the protagonist singing 'I did it, MY WAY !!' as he is borne to safety.

Tim had appeared in Edward Albees film 'Zoo Story' and acted in Jean Paul Sartre's 'No Exit'. He acted in plays for the Los Angeles Theatre Group which included Robbie Krieger of The Doors as a member. Tim said that he was also approached to play Woody Guthrie in Hal Ashby's film of Woody's early life 'Bound for Glory, the part ultimately went to David Carradine. It was later that we learned that Tim was wanted for the part of Arlo Guthrie, but this is very unlikely as Arlo was still a child during the time span of the film, it only covered Woody's early career as a traveller in search of success.

Another film titled 'Why' or 'Wild Orange' was filmed with Tim taking a cameo role alongside O.J.Simpson and Linda Gillen. At the time of the filming Tim was almost penniless he worked on the film for $420 per week. Roger McGuinn and Jacques Levy had almost completed their musical titled Gene Tryp which was based on Grieg's Peer Gynt. Their first choice for the lead part was Tim Buckley, but he died before the idea could be presented. In fact Tim often said in recorded interviews that he played guitar on The Byrds first album, McGuinn maintains that this was yet another of Tim's myth creating prevarications. In one interview Tim actually states that he played Roger McGuinn's solo on Mr Tambourine Man. Hal Bartlett's film 'Changes' did use Tim's music as it's soundtrack, and the earlier mentioned 'Coming Home' played the final credits to 'Once I Was'. Probably Tim's most memorable performance on film would be in edition No 26 of The Monkees' Television series. Tim sang 'The Song of the Siren' which would ultimately be recorded for the Starsailor album, albeit with a different melody.

After the release of the 'Look at the Fool' album Tim was soon back on tour in Texas and California, on what was to be his final live performances. In April 1975 Tim finally met his son Jeff who was now eight years old, they spent nine days together, two months later Tim had died. The night before his death Tim performed before an 1800 capacity audience at The Dallas Electric Ballroom.

On June 29th 1975 Tim visited an old friend Richard Keeling, Tim was already drunk when he arrived at Keeling's house. After some further drinking it is alleged that Keeling dared Tim to take some cocaine and set out a line for him to snort. Tim had been clean of drugs for some considerable time and thus had no hard-drug immunity. The drug was in fact heroin, it is evident that Tim was unaware just what he was taking up his nose. Keeling and an un-named woman took Tim home to wife Judy, she was used to seeing Tim inebriated, she thought that he might be faking, however this proved to be dissimilar to Tim's usual drunkenness. Tim's breathing became increasingly erratic and a concerned Judy summoned an ambulance. As Tim was taken away on the stretcher his final words to Judy were 'Bye Bye Baby'. Tim was pronounced dead on arrival at Santa Monica Hospital, California, an autopsy followed. For some unknown reason a few of the American Daily papers stated that Tim had died climbing the stairs of his house.

Tim would have been declared dead by misadventure by coroner Dr Joseph H.Choi but Richard Keeling's feelings of guilt later spilled out in conversation. Keeling was subsequently arrested and charged with first then second degree murder for supplying the drug. He finally pleaded guilty to involuntary manslaughter and served 120 days prison, to this was added a three year probationary period. A second death certificate was then issued for Tim Buckley.

Tim Buckley was cremated, Lee Underwood performed the eulogy at the service performed at The Wiltshire Funeral Home, Santa Monica. Tim was laying in an open coffin during the service, he was dressed in a black silk shirt, and he clasped a yellow orchid in his hands. Lee Underwood says that Tim's beard had grown considerably since he had been released from the autopsy. The funeral announcement card arranged for Thursday July 2nd 1975, included Alfred Lord Tennyson's sombre poem 'Crossing the Bar'. The last lines are 'I hope to see my pilot face to face, when I have crossed the bar'. Throughout the service the sounds of women weeping could be heard, many of his ex-lovers attended the funeral. Tim Buckley had created just nine albums in nine years.

Lee Underwood was extremely angry at Keeling's pose as a close friend to Tim Buckley. He considered that Keeling was always jealous of Tim, and because Tim was his usual obnoxious self when drunk he had given him heroin. Underwood adds that Tim was probably dared to take it, as usual Tim could never refuse a dare, ever. Lee Underwood adds as a suffix 'I hope Richard Keeling writhes in his guilt forever'.

Tim's only possessions were his guitar and his amplifier, he left many unpaid debts. Tim Buckley had everything in excess except success.

Larry Beckett gave up writing moved to Portland Oregon and became a computer executive, and ultimately very rich.

Road manager and close confidant Barry The Bear Shultz died in 1979 from cancer in up-State New York. He was extremely saddened by Tim's death, he said that 'Tim was frail but had no death wishes whatsoever'.

Lee Underwood became a writer and music reviewer, in his days with Tim on stage Lee would sit quietly on his stool playing his inspirational accompaniment. He released an album titled California Sigh (CS101) in May 1989, he has become a renowned expert on New Age Music.

After the death of writer Lillian Roxon in 1978, for some unknown reason the paragraphs concerning Tim Buckley were deleted from her Encyclopedia of Rock.

There are very few people throughout Tim's career who ever said word against him in print. Tim seems to have been smart, sweet, coy, kind, nasty, obnoxious (when drunk), a racist, a philanderer, and a loyal friend, he was just a one long series of contradictions. If Bob Dylan is 'The Blotting Paper Man' soaking up influences and ideas and transforming them to his own advantage, then Tim Buckley was 'The Vacuum Cleaner Man' he just inhaled personalities, sounds and influences and blew them straight back at the audience with his gymnastic vocal chords.

No single description of Tim Buckley's music is adequate, the earlier explorative albums were close to jazz, the songs were simple and perceptive, introspective and intimate. Tim was always on the verge of great popularity but many listeners considered the melodies too similar, with his personal indifference to the audience response often making the show mundane yet exquisite and unique.

'Memory is a wicked and treacherous temptress,
Tim Buckley held hands with the world for a while,
He burned with a very special flame.

Lee Underwood (Downbeat Magazine 1977)

THE LIVE RECORDINGS

All the live recording were released posthumously, Tim was preparing to record a double live set at the time of his death which would encompass his complete career. The live sets that have emerged are of varying quality, some are detailed below.

(a) THE PEEL SESSIONS
Released on Strange Fruit Label Classic Peel in 1991 and later as MORNING GLORY on The Band of Joy Label in 1994 including two additional tracks recorded for The Old Grey Whistle Test. When Clive Selwood (assisted by John Peel) set up Strange Fruit Records he said that one of the reasons was to ultimately release these tracks. Recorded on a wet Sunday morning Clive says, yet other articles seem to contend that it was a wet Saturday.

For John Peel's Top Gear Show.
MORNING GLORY (recorded 2nd April 1968/ Broadcast 7th April 1968).
The definitive version, pristine clean sound, Lee Underwood and Tim at their peak, this is so beautiful it will bring tears to the eyes of any Buckley fan.
COMING HOME TO YOU (Happy Time) (rec 2/4/68/Bdcst 7/4/68)
Carter Collins great on congas covering for the lack of a bass player admirably. Lee Underwood has rarely played such an accurate and thoughtful accompaniment.
SING A SONG FOR YOU (Rec 2/4/68/Bdcst 7/4/68)
Without Carter Collins congas but someone is playing what sounds like finger cymbals to accompany the two guitars.
HALLUCINATIONS/TROUBADOUR, (Rec 2/4/68/ Bdcst 7/4/68) two songs that are regularly segued together, congas and shakers are prevalent and Lee Underwood plays an extended though excellent guitar solo. The track has a duration of 10.5 minutes and may have been even longer.
ONCE I WAS, (Rec 2/4/68 /Bdcst 7/4/68) commences with an exasperated Tim Buckley saying "It's cool just tell Herbie (Cohen) to shut up and turn the thing on!". The congas are excellent as Tim asks us if we will ever remember him.

The book by Ken Garner that lists all Peel Sessions (In Session Tonight/BBC Books 1993/it included a free sampler CD) is at variance with the details on the Compact disc booklets. The date of recording is listed as 1/4/68, with Top Gear broadcast of 'Once I was' and 'Hallucinations' on 19/5/68.

The following two tracks are not on either compact disc but were also featured on a later John Peel programme.
LOVE FROM ROOM 109 (rec 1/10/68/Bdcst 13/10/68)is augmented by the addition of vibraphone. John Peel introduced the song as from room 170 and

this was then taken through to the Ken Garner, Peel Sessions book. It is likely that the song had not been given a final title at the time of the Peel recording. For some reason Clive Selwood did not think it pertinent to add this track to the compact disc, even with no waves lapping on the shore this is a very competent version.

THE TRAIN (rec 1/10/68/Bdcst 13/10/68) plays through un-announced at the completion of the song John Peel says that it was a new un-titled song. The version that appeared on Blue Afternoon has some different lyrics, but it is certainly the same song.

The Sessions book also states that BUZZIN FLY was recorded on 1/10/68 but I have been unable to locate a copy of the recording, perhaps the title presented in the Sessions book for The Train was Buzzin' Fly as no title was acknowledged at the time.

(b) THE OLD GREY WHISTLE TEST

DOLPHINS (Rec 21/5/74) has Charles Whitney (ex-Family) on guitar, Tim Hinkley on bass, and Ian Wallace on drums. The guitar is mixed far back into the mix, and Ian Wallace taps the cymbal for much of the time.

HONEYMAN (Rec 21/5/74) has Tim playing electric guitar alongside that of Charles Whitney, the overall feel is that it was a first and only un-rehearsed recording.

To digress slightly, the old grey whistle test itself (not the show) was the test performed by the songwriters of The Brill Building (New York) and Tin Pan Alley (London's, Denmark Street area) that decided if a song was easily memorable. The writer's would sing a song once completely through to 'old greys' who were in fact the grey haired lady cleaners of the building. If these women could then whistle the melody after they had finished then it was likely that it might be catchy enough to be a hit song. If you do this with Tim Buckley's songs then perhaps only a few would pass the test, now which do you think they might be? Strange Feeling, Buzzin' Fly and of course Morning Glory, but dear reader you might think differently.

(c) DANISH RADIO CONCERT 1968

Two tracks available on bootleg cassette, TRACK ONE is an untitled and unknown improvisation, some of the lyrics are from the incorrectly titled Strange Feeling from The Queen Elizabeth Hall 'Dream Letter' album. GYPSY WOMAN is more subdued than normal, Tim is most likely pronouncing his words more precisely to assist an audience listening in a language foreign to them. BUZZIN' FLY is again a clear version the audience loved both tracks as the applause indicates. STRANGE FEELING is still an embryonic song searching for the final set of lyrics. The bass player for this show was Nils

Henning, taking over from Danny Thompson, Tim introduces himself to an unsuspecting audience with "Hi, I'm the queen of the hop!"

(d) LIVE AT THE STARWOOD, Los Angeles 1975 (bootleg cassette)
The show is one half of a show from a weeks engagement at the club. Buzzin' Fly, Nighthawkin', Dolphins, Get on Top, and an extended Devil Eyes are included. The band consisted of Joe Falsia on guitar, Jeff Elrick on bass, Buddy Hamilton on drums and John Harrison on organ. It is the organ sound that make the this live show different. At the finale Tim says "Look out all you women working in your kitchens, Tim Buckley's back in town!" The individual performances are quite good but the recording is not, the tape hiss is so loud that it is tiresome.

(e) LIVE IN DETROIT 1975, (bootleg cassette) includes Blue Melody, Tijuana Moon, Sally Go Round the Roses, Helpless, Who Could Deny, Dolphins, an excellent untitled rocking instrumental which allows the band to flex their muscles, Nighthawkin', and Stone in Love. Once more the performance is very good but the quality of the recording is dreadful.

(f) LIVE AT THE TROUBADOUR   3rd and 4th September 1969
(Edsel/Bizarre/Straight Records 1994)
The cover depicts a pensive looking Tim sitting at the foot of a set of timber stairs. The booklet has an sunny alfresco photograph of Tim showing off his country and western red and white flowered shirt. The booklet discusses The Dream Letter double album released earlier, it is also mooted in the editorial that vibes are included on this live show, they are not in evidence, nor are they shown in the band credits. Art Tripp (ex-Zappa's Mothers/Beefheart's Magic Band/Mallard) is on drums and John Balkin was on bass.

STRANGE FEELING is pleasant and is followed by an inconsequential instrumental 'Venice Mating Call' (subtitled by Tim at the microphone as 'All we are saying is give smack a chance). I DON'T NEED THE RAIN is presented as a new song yet it uses the lyric from 'Nobody Walkin' (Lorca), he says 'I am so happy I will let you come home, you have been out turning tricks on the Avenue'. I HAD A TALK WITH MY WOMAN also has a second announced title from Tim this he calls 'I love you so much honey I could shit!'. During the song Tim adds a nuance that is new when he whistles the tune. GYPSY WOMAN after Tim provides his initial squeals and wails it is nearly three minutes before he sings. The gypsy woman continues to hypnotise and cast her spell on him, the duration of the song (12.5 minutes plus 1 minute applause) allows for a series of jazz solos, the interminable conga solo, and then Tim returns to bark and wail at the audience with plenty of his gymnastic throat vocals. BLUE MELODY is wonderful and is one of the best performances of the song. CHASE THE BLUES AWAY is Tim's song for breaking down the barriers with a woman, take away her fears, convince her that he will touch her body like a breeze passing by. DRIFTIN' has the great sensuous sentiments 'When there is wine in your belly, love rhythms on your tongue, for you are a woman and each of your men has been too young'. Finally NOBODY WALKIN' has Lee Underwood switching to play electric piano which has a 'fuzz' button depressed or perhaps was recorded too close to the microphone, once more the percussion solo goes on for twice the required length but completes a great compilation from the two Troubadour shows.

(g) LIVE FROM THE BOARDING HOUSE SAN FRANCISCO 1972, is yet another bootleg tape where the sound Of Tim Buckley is masked by plenty of tape hiss. GYPSY WOMAN is given a long an uneventful rendition, the long conga drum solo is followed by an interminable duet between Tim and the congas once more. Tim just never knew when to stop, surely he must have realised how restless the audience were becoming, it can be heard as the recording seems to come from a tape recorded set in the middle of the audience. MORNING GLORY follows and sounds more like ROOM 109 ISLANDER as it is taken at a snails pace. CHASE THE BLUES AWAY is much better and is possibly the definitive version. In the introduction of THE DOLPHINS, Tim refers to Fred Neil as his one and only friend.

(h) HONEYMAN LIVE FOR RADIO WLIR 27th November 1973.
(Edsel Records 1995)
The Sefronia band sounds fully rehearsed on this recording, there is very little improvisation. The album included pristine clear production of THE DOLPHINS, BUZZIN' FLY and GET ON TOP. We are also presented with the definitive version of DEVIL EYES, this is due to the band, Joe Falsia plays some superb guitar breaks, Buddy Helm' s driving force drumming, and Mark Tiernan filling all the gaps with his electric piano playing. For once in a live performance Tim's wailing and shrieking vocalese is perfectly complimented by the band. An ordinary version of PLEASANT STREET is followed by SALLY GO ROUND THE ROSES.

I have always wondered why Tim insisted on singing this traditional folk-round, he does nothing with it and it is so repetitive. STONE IN LOVE is again a perfect setting for a Joe Falsia wonderful but very short guitar solo. HONEYMAN is taken as a walking blues that goes on too long. SWEET SURRENDER has a sedate opening led by Mark Tiernan's electric piano, this song has the splendid reference to a tall girl as 'His flamingo loved to tango'. Altogether this release is complimentary to what went previously, worth buying to hear Tim playing with a rehearsed band, and thankfully the 15 minute Gypsy Eyes is missing.

(h) DREAM LETTER LIVE LONDON 7th OCTOBER 1968 (The album sleeve states 10th July 1968 due to the fact that in the USA the month is written first, the box of tapes was designated 10/7/1968)
(Demon/Enigma Records 1990)

Last but most certainly not least is this wonderful double album. I have saved this till last for two reasons,

(i) I was there working in security and can add a few extra pieces of information which I have saved for this album review

(ii) This is one of the finest live albums ever, and thus is a fitting way to complete the story of Tim Buckley.

Peter Drummond at the time an innovative disc jockey on Radio One BBC was asked to introduce Tim, he had paid for his seat and was about to sit down when asked to perform this function. Drummond to my ears was the Number two BBC Disc Jockey at the time behind John Peel, Drummond's Saturday show introduced so many wonderful new american acts.

The show opens with BUZZIN' FLY, and PHANTASMAGORIA IN TWO, and they are used as looseners and played competently. MORNING GLORY is introduced by Tim as a song of a hobo beating up a college kid outside Dallas, he certainly meant inspired by that premise. A sublime version of Fred Neil's DOLPHINS follows it would many years before it finally was recorded by Tim in a studio for the Sefronia album.

I'VE BEEN OUT WALKING uses a first line that was to be re-used by Jackson Browne in 1973 for his own 'These days'. The line is 'I've been out walking, ain't done much talking, these days'. The Jackson Browne lyric was actually quoted many years earlier by Tom Nolan in his 'Orange County Three' article for Cheetah Magazine, so it was obviously a lyric idea that both singers used at some time. Tim's song is of deep loneliness, he has wanted so long to see her, to pay back the debts that he owes her, yet he hasn't got the heart or time to tell her. He hasn't got the answers she came to hear. After the show I was near enough to a confidant of Tim's to ask a question about this track and another which appears later on the album. It was clear to me that when Tim was singing this song (and probably many others later in his career) he had a melody fixed in his mind and was improvising words. My question was 'Ask Tim if he was thinking of 'When Will I be Loved', by the Everly Brothers whilst he sang this song ?' I watched the man speak to Tim, the man pointed me out as if to say 'Him over there'. Tim smiled pointed at me and said " One out of two is not bad". If you read farther you will learn what the second question was.

THE EARTH IS BROKEN another new song which never got a studio recording. A gentle song sung solo, it has sentiments for the under-dog hanging in an attempt to save the Earth's environment. The sun is not clear any more, the rivers are not clean, Tim's ecological song, he yearns for the cleansing of a planet becoming polluted. Tim makes the lyric personal by adding 'The letters came to lonesome Timmy, when a woman was younger she knew what to do, now that is not so any more'. In the lyric Tim mentions his friend Larry Beckett as his brother who has been taken away. Larry had been drafted into the U.S. Army at the time. I think that this song is based on the old scottish folk song 'Westering Home' although it is also an american folk song that I cannot recall. This was my second question which Tim confirmed one as correct. This may not be the exact melody line but it is very close. I have always thought it strange that this ability to create lyrics whilst playing guitar chords different to the song in Tim's mind, had never been mooted to him in any interview, ever.

WHO DO YOU LOVE, is one of the songs that I never heard at the show, I was busy. When I received the album I quite expected it to be a version of the hit song from the Philadelphia group The Sapphires but it is entirely different. Remember the good times, forget the rain. This has the feel of an Odetta spiritual, Tim taps his guitar to create the percussion which is not part of the group. Tim also uses parts of the song 'Green Rocky Road' (Fred Neil) and segues it into the title line of 'Run Shake a Life' (Ritchie Havens). On this track Danny Thompson on bass sounds totally bemused by his lack of rehearsal, he is barely audible throughout the track, playing so quietly and stopping.

PLEASANT STREET is Tim playing solo once more, the song of the exploitation of the true hippies by the commercial charlatans. YOU KEEP ME HANGING ON, is Tim Buckley plays the Supremes, the Holland Dozier Holland song played with some force both in the voice and in the guitar strumming. LOVE FROM ROOM 109, taken at a faster pace than the studio (and other live recordings) version. This is beautiful as a solo without the waves from the studio version and without the tape hiss.

STRANGE FEELIN' is the incorrect title for the song, apparently it should have been 'Mockingbird', it is a different song to the track of the same title that appeared on the 'Happy Sad' album. Tim starts with 'Hush don't say a word' as does the Inez Foxx hit version from 1963. It is not that song either but possibly Tim was influenced by the lyric. Old men are constantly mentioned and young girls, he knows the girls well and gives them candy from the corner store, he also gets his religion from books. The man in the song is also looking from his window at the school girls, a man with a fixation perhaps. The chorus asks for her not to weep fret or moan, when in love the sunshine will warm your heart. A mockingbird is singing on the hill side and the whippoorwills are calling. The advice to the girls from Tim is don't marry the milkman because he gets around, nor the factory-man because he comes home dirty, or the mail-man because he is always late. This song may have been improvised in the performance, and was never given a studio version.

CARNIVAL SONG, is noted as a track on the album incorrectly, it does not appear. The following track 'Hi Lilly, Hi Lo' is a carnival song from the film 'Lili'. The title is different 'Lilly' in lieu of 'Lili', and the song has very few features from the original written by Helen Deutsch for the 1952 Leslie Caron Mel Ferrer film. That song was also a hit for Richard (Dr Kildare) Chamberlain in 1963. Tim introduces the song by saying " If you are ever in New York there are not many carnivals going on. That may not mean much if you are used to a carnival, once in a while I write a carnival song, what is a song without a carnival'. He then sings HI LILLY, HI LO. The band creates a carousel waltz tune, Tim sings his own song the only similarity with the original is that towards the end he uses the line from the original 'The song of love is a sad song'. The song publishers gave Helen Deutsch a share of the royalties for Tim's song.

HALLUCINATIONS has yet another subtitle it was 'I love you so much honey I could shit', but now Tim adds 'Santa's got a plastic mojo'. The tuning takes so long that Tim quips pointing at the wood of his guitar, "Well you know how long the tree took to grow". The band flexes out a little during the song with David Friedman's vibes creating the psychedelic effect. TROUBADOUR is given a beautiful folky version which leads into DREAM LETTER. This song has the line 'Sleep inside my dreams tonight', and includes Tim's feeling of guilt at the end of his first marriage, he had been fighting his own wars, probably with the demon drink. The melody uses a nursery rhyme probably 'See Saw Marjorie Dawe'. 'Blue Afternoon's' HAPPY TIME received it's first airing here and is warmly received by the audience.

WAYFARING STRANGER is a powerful song sung (as far as I know) on this show only. Tim is presenting his version of Bob Dylan's 'With God on Our Side', coupled with the Jews searching for their home. The stranger travels through the world alone, he finds sickness, toil and danger everywhere he goes. He is searching for his brother over Jordan's river, it will be his new home. It is necessary to go through the pain of happiness before you can finally smile. It is not what you spend, it is what you lend. Men will stand side-by-side bound for glory on freedom's side. Tim has rarely used so many different themes in one song, it does make for some deep concentrated listening. The song segues into YOU KEEP ME RUNNING which uses lyrics from Little Richard's 1956 rocker 'Slippin' and a Slidin'. Tim makes a denigrating statement concerning his feelings for himself, that would prove sadly accurate 'I am here on borrowed time, I'm just a rusty hinge'. The audience loved these two songs, there are understandable calls of 'more', it is the penultimate track and the highlight of a brilliant show.

The last track is ONCE I WAS, the premonitionary title for a song and a life, once he was and will never be again. This concludes one of the greatest live album sets by a singer-songwriter, this added to the sadness makes it all the more desperate that such a talented flame should have been extinguished so early.

We are still awaiting the emergence of the songs sung on two television programmes. Tim sang on 'Late Night Line-up' and 'The Julie Felix Show', but so far nobody has the recordings available for release, the video for the Julie Felix is thought to have been over-taped but hopefully someone else tape recorded Tim's songs for posterity.

There were two other official posthumous releases, both collections of previously released tracks.
THE BEST OF TIM BUCKLEY (Rhino Records RNLP 112, 1983)
THE LATE GREAT TIM BUCKLEY (Warner Records 250770-1, 1984)

ACKNOWLEDGEMENTS

David Boobbyer for his kind help in locating some rare tracks.
Articles letters and writings from Lee Underwood, John Platt, Andy Childs,
Scott Isler, Martin Ashton,
and last but not least for his encouragement Tony Coleman.

The following magazines and periodicals included articles that were used for reference:-

Zig Zag, Downbeat, The Washingtonian, Goldmine, Bucketfull of Brains, Rolling Stone, New Musical Express, Melody maker, Wire, Q, The Musician, Mojo, Sounds, The New York Times.

NO REPLY

The words and music of
NICK DRAKE

PAUL BARRERA

AGENDA

Agenda Ltd
Units 8/9 Kenyon's Trading Estate,
Weyhill Road, Andover, Hampshire, U.K., SP10 3NP

ONCE HE WAS The Tim Buckley Story
NO REPLY The Nick Drake Story

First Published May 1997

ISBN 1 899882 55 3

ONCE UPON A TIME

I have been reserved all my life...;
and I have only been able to let myself go
in certain situations.

Gabriel Faure (1845-1924)

Rodney and Molly Drake were living in Pakistan when their daughter Gabrielle was born. Rodney had taken a position working in the far east for a lumber company. He enjoyed the travel and living with the ex-patriate community abroad. His wife Molly had previously been a singer and loved listening to music. The lumber company abroad had many branches and this meant that the family regularly moved this time to Rangoon, Burma. It was here that their son was born, Nick Drake arrived on the 19th June 1948. The wandering had not finished and once more the family was up-rooted and moved to Bombay.

The family returned to England in 1950 and set up home in Tanworth-in-Arden. This sleepy village in the heart of Shakespeare country, not far from Stratford-upon-Avon and Redditch, with the nearest large town being Birmingham. Their dream house was named 'Far Leys' it was large and detached, built in 1912.

Nick's parents were upper middle class and the family unit was happy and conducive for allowing children to pursue their desires. Molly wrote songs herself although it does seem that none were ever published. Due to all the members of the household enjoying music the home was often filled with sound catering for the various musical tastes. Nick could regularly be observed conducting the music that was playing from the radio.

Nick was an achiever, he had the natural ability and mental faculties to succeed with little effort. From the age on 13 he attended Marlborough Public School. At school he learned basic piano, saxophone and clarinet. He became a prefect and head boy in his class. He was already 6'-0" tall and he became an excellent short distance runner. He set the school record for the 100 yards which is unlikely to be beaten, the school changed the race to 100 metres two years after Nick set his time. He went on to win the title for the 100 yards in The Wiltshire Amateur Athletic Championships.

He was always shy and quiet, whilst sister Gabrielle was gregarious Nick had trouble making friends, however he was never disliked. He was a loner which should not be confused with lonely they are in may ways opposites. A loner chooses to be alone. Gradually Nick's tastes in music changed, he was becoming more interested in the music of the time, it was now 1965. Nick visited London to hear rhythm and blues, he went to The Flamingo Club where the emerging band was The Blue Flames headed by Georgie Fame. Nick also went to The Marquee to see Stevie Winwood who was then vocalist for The Spencer Davis Band. Nick was also listening to The Graham Bond Organisation, Bond's version of 'St James' Infirmary Blues' was a particular favourite. Bob Dylan was invading the psyche of a generation at the time, Nick repeatedly played the album 'Bringing it all back Home' he especially liked the track 'She Belongs to Me'.

After repeated requests Rodney Drake finally purchased a £13.00 guitar for Nick, he could not put it down, he was a natural, and very soon he was playing it well. He continually practised sometimes all through the night. He also continued with his piano playing which was influenced by Mose Allison, who in turn had influenced Georgie Fame. At a school concert Nick played Mose Allison's 'Parchman Farm' on the piano. On guitar the first song that he would play for singalong purposes was 'Michael Row the Boat ashore' which had been a hit for The Highwaymen and Lonnie Donegan.

Many years later I would be seated at The Roundhouse in London where I had gone with my friend to see Country Joe McDonald, at this show an unknown singer guitarist emerged in the early hours of the morning, walking round-shouldered onto the stage sat on a stool and played. This was Nick Drake, the reason for adding this so early in this book is because my friend a good guitarist himself made a statement that I have always remembered. Nick's playing was reasonable but the singer was detaching himself from the audience, he was playing for himself and not for the audience. We were sitting a little way back, the tunes were ordinary, the lyrics hard to understand, I don't mean they were inaudible but a lyric sheet would have been necessary for adequate comprehension. The tunes were not instant. My friend said "That guitarist is probably self taught he has not been shown how to tune the instrument properly". He also remarked how lucky Nick was to have such long fingers. In fact the guitar was tuned to assist Nick's own innovative style of playing . The guitar was 'Guild M-20, once Nick had learned a song and the tuning he sang it on every occasion in exactly the same manner. These unusual tunings were to become an important part of Nick Drake's appeal. We never realised at the time but this was Nick's first professional performance.

Nick was intelligent he had earlier won a place at Fitzwilliam College, Cambridge, he was there to study English. He continued with his guitaring and became a student that rarely attended lectures, he preferred to spend his time with music. During the holiday break in 1967 aged 19 Nick went to Provence in France where he learned conversational French, he also travelled to Morocco and remained there for nearly four months until the start of the following college term. It was whilst Nick was in Morocco that he wrote his first song, or more accurately the first song that he thought was good enough to sing for others. The song 'Strange Meeting II' it would not be released on an album until after Nick had died.

Nick continued to be a loner, but all the people who knew him remember him as a kind and friendly youth, even in this time of his life his verbal communication skills were not great. His music tastes moved slightly he was impressed by Tim Buckley (Goodbye and Hello), Van Morrison (Astral Weeks), Jim Webb's collaboration with The Fifth Dimension on their album 'Magic Garden', and Randy Newman (First, eponymously titled album).

It is pertinent to note here that of all the singer songwriters that have come and gone over the years the closest in compositional style to Nick Drake would be Tim Buckley. Nick's close friends at the time were Brian Wells and Paul Wheeler. Wheeler was also writing songs and Nick and Paul would each listen each other's latest compositions. All three friends enjoyed the songs of Jackson C. Frank, and Nick recorded some of Frank's songs onto his home tape recorder. Paul Wheeler wrote the song 'Give Us a Ring' which John Martyn later recorded on his 'Road to Ruin' album.

Nick continued his English studies for a further two years, he read Verlaine and Rimbaud two writers whose lives were interlinked, they were lovers for many years. More songs were being created which were played to the other students, none seem to be over whelmed by the quality of what they were hearing. Nick made a tape at home which consisted of twelve songs, some self-compositions but most were versions of songs composed by others. The tape was made available to enthusiasts after Nick had died but it is relevant for the sake of chronology to review the tracks here.

MY SUGAR SO SWEET (Trad arranged Nick Drake) is a gentle blues. GET TOGETHER (Perry Miller a.k.a.,Jesse Colin Young) a hit for Jesse Young's group The Youngbloods in 1969. Written in 1967 it got a second lease of life when the song became the theme tune for The National Council of Christians & Jews. Nick sings it like a gentle ballad, the song has subsequently become a rocker of some power with various groups providing versions. Dino Valente also laid claim to this song but it is registered to J.C.Young.

DON'T THINK TWICE IT'S ALRIGHT (Bob Dylan) is sung faster than Dylan's original, Nick sounds a little like Tom Paxton on this version. IF YOU LEAVE ME PRETTY MAMA (Trad Arr Nick Drake) is a good rolling blues, the sentiments are if you leave me I will forget about you, but after tomorrow night.

73

COURTING BLUES (Bert Jansch) is taken from Bert Jansch's first eponymously titled album. It is reputed to be the first song Bert ever wrote. It was for his girl-friend at the time Elizabeth Cruikshanks. STROLLING DOWN THE HIGHWAY (Jansch) is also from Bert's first album which he recorded into a tape recorder on his kitchen table. For some reason the artists who have provided their versions prefer to title the song 'Strollin' omitting the 'G' which is included on Bert's album sleeve notes.

BLUES RUN THE GAME (Jackson C.Frank) a song eventually sung by the world and his wife, hardly a troubadour anywhere fails to sing this song from Frank's album. WINTER IS GONE (Trad arr Nick Drake) is an average song which has all the hallmarks of later Nick Drake compositions. HERE COME THE BLUES (Jackson C.Frank) also from Frank's album, there were so many copies of this album in London at the time. It was impossible to attend a party anywhere without this album being found somewhere in the pile of records. ALL MY TRIALS (Soon be over) (Trad arr Nick Drake) a duet sung with sister Gabrielle, she seems to struggle a little with the key signature, but it would make a nice family recording, but little more. The negro spiritual has been sung by artists such as Odetta, Harry Belafonte, Steve Miller, and Paul McCartney, and thousands more.

TOMORROW'S SUCH A LONG TIME (Bob Dylan) a competent version of one of Dylan's less popular songs. COCAINE BLUES (Luke Jordan) Although Luke Jordan first recorded the song as a version of Julius Daniels 'Crow Jane Blues' in 1927, 'Cocaine Blues was registered by Reverend Gary Davis to Chandos Music and thus he became the acknowledged composer. Davis had recorded the song for Prestige Records, Jackson Browne provided a superb version on his 'Running on Empty' album.

MILK AND HONEY (Jackson C.Frank) the third song on this early tape taken from the Jackson C. Frank album, there are more details of Jackson C.Frank in the chapter concerning the artists that influenced Nick Drake. SUMMERTIME (George and Ira Gershwin) receives a gentle version, BLACK MOUNTAIN (Trad arr Nick Drake) shows just how expert Nick was becoming on the guitar.

RAIN / OUR SEASON (Nick Drake) a song that had no title so two have been chosen. The lyrics are average, they mention our season with the rain, leaves, flowers, and our love in the rain. Many poets seem drawn to the rain as a method of washing away all the problems, here Nick knows that lovers in the rain feel only warmth, and it influences one's dreams. I understand the gist of the lyrics but I'm unsure if they are in any way believable. Rain was to figure in a number of Nick Drake songs, in many as an omen of darkness.

74

BIRD FLEW BY (Nick Drake) if this really is one of Nick's earliest compositions then he already is showing the hallmarks of depression. Once more it is the seasons and nature, most of Nicks songs at the time were based on rural themes. Nick is constantly asking what is point of the seasons. 'A list of crumpled broken hearts comes from the need to play so many parts'. Already he feels that too much is being asked of him and he is yet to make his foray into the music industry. 'The wind and the rain shook hands again, untouched by the World they managed to stay sane', these lyrics are particularly relevant with hindsight. But it is the line 'Your life flies away as the night turns to day' that are so pertinent. This song would require some considerable engineering expertise applied to it before it could be released, but it might be worth the effort.

TO THE GARDEN (Nick Drake) as extra reverb on the vocal, for yet another rural song. There is a song 'Garden of the Moon' written by Al Dubin, Johnny Mercer, and Harry Warren, in 1938. The song was sung by Mabel Todd in the film 'Garden of the Moon'. I am informed that there are similarities but it seems that Nick has re-arranged it and added some of his own lyrics. I could not locate a copy of the song to be sure, but the cassette of these home recordings does have a question mark in the composers parenthesis. I personally think that these lyrics are totally Nick Drake. The sentiments are that she could not come into the garden, but she said that she may join them there soon. I can't imagine Johnny Mercer writing 'The sky too wide to see the blind man' or 'In floating thoughts she'd sway'. Whatever the truth the song is another lost masterpiece enveloped in tape hiss.

STRANGE MEETING II (Nick Drake) and JOEY (Nick Drake) are competent versions of songs recorded later.

BLOSSOM (Nick Drake) is a song that Robert Kirby would mention in an interview, he liked this love song so much he feels it should have been recorded on an album. Not one of Nick's more accomplished lyrics. Lines like 'Trees came alive, Bees left their hive' would never have been used on later songs. Again Nick is using the scenes from his window, he hopes that the change of seasons will bring a change of fortune, a new love. Many of Nick's songs at the time had references to the seasonal changes, living the life of a country boy would certainly have been the motivation.

BEEN SMOKING TOO LONG, was apparently written by a friend of Nick's, and a good track it is to finish the home recordings, this would later be cleaned-up by the engineer for inclusion on Nick's posthumous album, 'Time of No Reply'.

Nick appeared at the Cambridge May Ball in 1968 he was backed by a twelve piece female string orchestra all wearing black evening dresses, and white feather boas. During this performance Nick's microphone went dead, he continued to the end of the song unaware that anything had happened. The songs he sang included 'River Man' and 'Time has Told Me'. The orchestration for Nick's songs had been arranged by Robert Kirby. He was surprised to be asked, he was not a friend of Nick's, apparently Nick had been advised that he would be able to do the songs justice. This association would carry through Nick's career, the two men would drink and enjoy life together, there were few signs of the darkness that was yet to come.

FIVE LEAVES LEFT (Island ILPS 9105, 1969)

Delight must be the basis and aim of this art.
Simple melody clear rhythm

Giaochino Rossini (1792-1868)

Nick managed to be included on the bill of a charity show at The Roundhouse in North London. He sang quietly and played his guitar as a supporting act for Country Joe McDonald. The show was to raise funds for 'Peace in Vietnam', I have always wondered just where the money went for such a cause, especially as it was to contest a war against the strongest nation on Earth.

Nick's performance was introverted, I never noticed any of the charisma that other people saw in this singer who seemed to cover himself in a carapace and took little heed to the audience. Contrary to many opinions Nick never held the attention of the audience they were chatting amid plenty of calls for hush. His songs were not instant, in his career few of the songs ever were. It was at this concert that Ashley Tyger Hutchins the bass player for The Fairport Convention observed the lonely but different Nick Drake on stage.

The Fairport Convention were managed by Joe Boyd an american from Boston. He also had control of John and Beverly Martyn, The Incredible String Band, and The Pink Floyd. Joe Boyd a man deeply into quality new music met a wealthy american at a London nightclub, offered some funds Boyd decided to form his own company. The company name came from a line of a song written by Donovan 'Beatniks out to make it rich, must be the Season of the Witch', 'Witchseason' was thus created. Joe Boyd admitted that Witchseason was created predominantly to produce Pink Floyd, but it never did. Joe Boyd had been manager at London's U.F.O. club for a while and he had met and observed many of the up and coming singers and groups. Strangely he signed the recording rights of another of his groups The Incredible String Band over the Jac Holzman at Elektra, Holzman was producing Tim Buckley at the time.

Ashley Hutchins advice concerning Nick Drake was taken by Joe Boyd and a tape of home recordings was duly sent to Joe Boyd at Witchseason. The tape impressed Boyd and he decided to proceed with a studio recording. Joe Boyd also wished to have a company that provided all the necessary services for new artists. He now had a company responsible for publishing, management, production, advertising, and recording. He was well trusted and liked and seems he only had differences with his artists over the direction that they should take. He was a caring man but like all businessmen he needed to make a profit to survive. He found that he was now working 18 hour days and thus putting himself under considerable stress. Nick Drake would become his personal favourite artist, when he finally sold Witchseason to Island some time later there was a proviso in the contract that Nick Drake should be nurtured.

Sound Technique Studios was engineered and managed by John Wood, his relationship with Joe Boyd was excellent and eventually nearly all John Wood's time was taken by acts from Witchseason Productions Ltd. A small logo of a witch on a broomstick was included on each cover and advertising flyer, it became an endorsement to record purchaser of quality for the emerging group of British musicians.

Nick Drake visited Sound Techniques in Chelsea London in July 1968 and recorded the tracks that would ultimately become his first album. The recording was not completed in one session, far from it, the tracks were recorded two at a time. A gap of six weeks passed before another couple of tracks were laid down, finally ten were selected for release on the first album. Some of the tracks Joe Boyd and Nick decided should be enhanced by an orchestral backing. Joe Boyd requested that the up and coming orchestrator Richard Hewson provide his ideas for accompaniment. On hearing them Joe Boyd and John Wood thought they were alright, however Nick Drake thought differently. The arrangements were discarded by Nick in an inconsiderate and cavalier fashion, they were not what he could hear in his head.

At the time Nick was continuing his studies at Cambridge but was becoming increasingly alienated against university studies, he wanted a career in music. An exasperated Joe Boyd who had been surprised by Nick's dislike of Richard Hewson's arrangements asked Nick what he would suggest as a solution. Nick said that he knew a man in Cambridge who might be able to do them in the manner he wanted. When Joe Boyd asked what experience the man had, Nick responded with a short answer 'None'. Robert Kirby was surprised and flattered to be asked, Nick would just say to him 'In this part I hear oboes, here a flute, there some strings' and Kirby took it from there. It is not clear if Witchseason then paid for Robert Kirby to provide the arrangements. In an interview Kirby confirmed that the arrangement for 'Way to Blue', 'Thoughts of Mary Jane', 'When Day is Done' and 'Time of No Reply' had already been prepared for Nick's earlier college concerts.

Robert Kirby duly arrived at Sound Techniques and the required orchestra which had been requested in advance was ready and waiting. Whilst John Wood and Joe Boyd sat in the sound room, Kirby went from instrument to instrument asking and cajoling them to play their parts solo. Boyd and Wood were becoming increasingly mystified, they were setting up microphones and taking sound volumes of the musicians as they rehearsed, they were anticipating a disaster. Nick sat quietly confident. Finally Kirby indicated that they were ready to commence. The orchestra played; Joe and John looked at each other and said "Oh What!", it was beautiful, perfect, sublime. Apparently Nick recorded the track simultaneously with the orchestra rather than the usual style of over-dubbing the orchestra later.

Nick decided to leave university. His father Rodney suggested that perhaps he was making a mistake and should reconsider. Most parents would have given the same advice, 'If the music profession fails then at least you would have a university degree to rely on for later life.' Nick decided that he had to leave and with nine months of his degree course remaining, moved to London. He found and shared a flat in the cosmopolitan area of Notting Hill, but soon moved to a flat in Hampstead and lived alone.

The first album still required a title, 'Five Leaves Left' was selected, it was taken from the reminder slip enclosed in every packet of Rizla and Job cigarette papers. Ominously it was five leaves, one leaf for every year of Nick's remaining life.

Nick recorded an appearance on John Peel's programme Top Gear. The tracks were recorded the day before the show which was on 6th August 1969. Nick recorded four songs at The BBC Maida Vale Studios 'Time of No Reply, Cello Song, River man, and Three Hours'. The production engineers at the studio were Mike Harding and Pete Ritzema. (information from Ken Garner's book 'In Session Tonight' the complete Radio One recordings/BBC Books). The consensus of opinion is that these tracks were wiped clean and recorded-over, but hope exists that they may one day be located. So far these recordings have not emerged in bootleg form, so it seems unlikely that anyone had 'home-taped' the session from their radio.

FIVE LEAVES LEFT, was released on Island Records ILPS 9105/1969), and sold only 5000 copies. The cover designed by Diogenic Attempts Ltd is viridian green and includes a Keith Morris photograph of Nick looking out of a window. This photograph was not taken at his own flat in Hampstead but at a friends. John Morris took a series of pictures of Nick leaning up against a wall observing various people walking past. The one selected has a mildly amused Nick looking at a man hurrying by. The world races by and the artist stands and observes.

The voice of Nick is an hybrid of Peter Sarstedt and Donovan but ultimately instantly recognisable as that of Nick Drake. All the songs on this album were self composed.

TIME HAS TOLD ME, is a world weary blues, augmented by Richard Thompson on electric guitar, Danny Thompson on bass, and Paul Harris on piano. Joe Boyd explained that the piano was added later. The song is two separate poems. The second poem repeated twice becomes the chorus. On the first chorus it does seem as though Nick is singing 'Leave the ways that are making me 'Laugh'' rather than 'love', although it is definitely 'Love' on the repetition chorus. This is a song of self reassurance, 'Time' has told him that he is a 'rare find', a sentiment that all fans will acknowledge as correct. On this first ever song on a Nick Drake album we are informed that he wants a cure for a troubled mind.

RIVER MAN has a beautiful arrangement in 5/4 time by The Harry Robinson strings. Robinson had provided the backing band for a few Television Rock 'n Roll shows, he was the creator of the Lord Rockingham's XI band which had massive hits for Decca with 'Hoots Mon' and Wee Tom'. Here he has used ideas probably from Ravel for this quite beautiful arrangement, there are similarities in the song with the Kink's 'Sunny Afternoon'. One wonders why Robinson was not asked to score the other tracks on the album. The guitar picking style makes it difficult to hear the last of the five beats. Nick also introduces us to Betty whoever she is on this song. Betty suffers the same as Nick, pain in the mind, which may of course be migraine. The song is of outstanding beauty, for many Drake followers this is their favourite song, it one of the most immediate. The song probably concerns spiritualism or perhaps mysticism, at least The River Man is a good listener, and then tells all he knows. A superb song that explains in the last line how problems of any kind come and go just like a river.

THREE HOURS (mistitled as 'Sundown' on the initial release). It is apparent that three hours is important for everything. On this track Nick he sounds like his friend John Martyn. As the sun dies in the west the subject of the song, Jacomo, will have little need of shading the sun from his eyes flying east from the city at sundown. Danny Thompson is again on bass and additional conga drums are augmenting the backing played by Rocki Dzidzornu. Reviewers stated that the subject of the song was an eternal seeker, a lad named Jacomo, searching for enlightenment which is proving elusive inside three hours, it just takes three hours to achieve a task.

WAY TO BLUE is a song of general observations. It includes the first Robert Kirby arrangement on the album. Slow languid and beautiful, the deep cello bowing under the third line of the lyric is masterful, and so simple. A quest for knowledge, assuming that 'Blue' in the song is some condition of nirvana. The answer seems un-attainable the question is still being asked as the song ends.

DAY IS DONE is similar to the previous track, a song of general observations. Robert Kirby's arrangement has some extraordinary similarities to the synthesized strings of Gordon Marron on the 1968 'United States of America' album. The album one of the greatest from the late 1960s was produced and sung by Joseph Byrd. Nick Drake's guitar is creating a baroque harpsichord effect. The sentiments are for when one's time is up on Earth. Nick uses The day, The Race, The Hope, The Game, The Bird, and The Party. When they are all finished then life ends, or perhaps it is just, The Day.

CELLO SONG a song that was mixed and re-mixed many times. Clare Lowther provides the cello on this track which also includes bass and congas, a slightly ethnic-Indian sound is created. The first line is almost 'Amazing Grace', Nick's guitaring is so brilliant that it fills the sound panorama completely. John Wood was placing four microphones in an arc in front of Nick, and a fifth farther away to pick up the studio ambience, it certainly worked admirably. The cello motif is played and replayed regularly throughout the song, at the coda Nick hums the same notes. The song gradually recedes, the cello stops and the congas and shakers play through to the end. The track and the vocal has the sound and feel of Marc Bolan and Steve Peregrine Took in their Tyrannosaurus Rex days. The sentiments are a meditation for leaving things behind, for sleeping away one's problems in dreams. The World is cruel, the night is cold, just sit and sing a song and then drift away to the clouds.

THE THOUGHTS OF MARY JANE, is another masterful Robert Kirby arrangement. A song in the Ralph McTell mould as he sang of his Factory Girl. The strings only join the song at the end of the second verse, and then they proceed to grow until they threaten to over power Nick. The flute introduction is perfect as is the song, one of Nick Drakes best ever songs. Nick continues to sing of the sky, the rain, and this strange World. If Mary Jane is just sitting quietly then nobody will know her thoughts, later Nick would sit and do the exact same thing.

MAN IN A SHED consists of four simple descending chords. The piano of Paul Harris was added by Joe Boyd whilst in New York, strangely it is over Nick's guitar break. The story of a madman living in seclusion out of the rain. If the moon creates a lunatic then what does the rain create ? The man is in love with a lady of considerable means, does he stand a chance in gaining her affection ? Will she leave the grand house and live in his decaying shed? Does Nick actually say 'Her shed' when he visited her, it does seem a more likely reason for visiting. (On the demo versions he says 'His' as on the lyric sheet). The song ends optimistically when they shed up together, (or should that be 'shack' up together), and at last stop the rain, or the problems of the World falling on (or through) his head.

FRUIT TREE, a song that mother Molly Drake enjoyed very much, the uncredited oboe player who is part of Robert Kirby's orchestra is superb. An autobiographical song of the search for fame and fortune. This is one of Nick's most poetic and thoughtful lyrics. It is likely that Nick had been reading William Blake at the time, Nick is presenting to us a stream of thoughts which indicate that fame is transparent, it is necessary to learn one's craft and base everything on a firm foundation. It is also pertinent that Nick mentions being remembered after death, 'Forgotten while you are here, remembered for a while'. The final two verses must have been an after thought, they really don't add anything to the lyric that had been sung earlier, perhaps Nick decided that the song just required some form of conclusion.

SATURDAY SUN, has a different sound due to the inclusion of Tristam Fry on vibraphone and drums. This recording draws parallels with Tim Buckley's recordings after David Friedman had joined on vibes. Nick is actually playing piano on this track. The song although of reasonable quality is probably the worst on the album. Working people always look forward to Saturday, and if the sun is shining then it is an added bonus. The surprise of the sun is once again killed by the rain, did Nick have a phobia for rain, it is fast becoming a recurring theme for causing seemingly insurmountable problems.

The album is wonderful, Kirby arranges with possibly George Frideric Handel in mind, Nick's eclecticism made him popular with the intellectuals that bothered to listen. This was a selection of songs that Nick had taken a lifetime to create, he hoped for wider recognition, the public at large ignored the album.

In September 1969 Nick opened the show for Fairport Convention, and John and Beverly Martyn at The Royal Festival Hall, London. Nick never spoke to the audience just sat and sang to a sell-out audience of 2500 people. His applause surprised him and he was ushered back onto the stage to sing an encore, he sang 'Things Behind the Sun' a song not included on the first two albums. The audience at The Festival Hall were well behaved and appreciative, this was not to be the situation in many smaller clubs. One of the worst was for The Coventry Climax Apprentices, the audience gave Nick a bad time, they wanted pop music. The quietness of Nick's performance meant that on many occasions the audiences returned to talking. If this upset Nick then he rarely gave any indication of the fact, he just lived inside his own world, and played his music.

BRYTER LAYTER (Island Records ILPS 9134, 1970)

*The composer who stumbles in taking a step forward
is worth more attention than the composer who shows us
how easily he can step backwards.*

Ernest Reyer (1823-1909)

Living in Hampstead Nick started writing the songs for his second album. He was more than a little upset by the lack of attention that the first album had received. Joe Boyd had given Nick a weekly stipend so that he would have money on which to live. Nick was continuing to play clubs arranged by Witchseason, it is alleged that Nick was only completely satisfied with three of his live performances.

Nick was becoming increasingly introverted, never a gregarious character he was considered reasonable company for most of the persons who spent their spare time with him. There are many people who have trouble in communicating, Nick's problem was not isolated. I never met Nick but I have met people who have what I consider the same problem. Some people can not bear silences either in conversation or on the telephone, they have to fill that void, they are embarrassed by the lack of sound. It is my guess that Nick was the opposite, I remember a close friend of mine who could sit in my car for two hours without speaking and yet was marvellous conversationalist when asked the questions and thus created the discourse. When I stopped speaking he stopped, he could not create a new dialogue, the silence meant nothing to him, he just returned to his natural contemplations. I think this particular person admired people who could commence discussions. The articles and interviews concerning Nick Drake certainly have parallels with this unfortunate uncommunicative situation.

BRYTER LAYTER, was recorded with members of Fairport Convention plus other musicians. Richard Thompson a brilliant guitarist stated that in the recording where he added guitar he and Nick never spoke to each other. Nigel Waymouth provided the photographs for the cover, Nick sitting holding the guitar showing off his sponge (or maybe crepe) soled bumper shoes. The orchestral arrangements were again by Robert Kirby, engineering by John Wood, produced for Witchseason by Joe Boyd. The early copies of the albums had a typing error that stated that Robert Kirby also provided 'bass' arrangements, that should have read 'brass'. The first album had been rural and rustic, this album was positively City. Nick had transferred us from 'The Man in the Shed' to the 'City clock'. The album was released in the U.S.A. as 'Nick Drake' on Island SMAS 9307.

83

INTRODUCTION an instrumental to lead in the album, not called 'The Overture' although that is the title provided by Robert Kirby in discussion on Swedish radio.

HAZEY JANE II, this is different due to the arrangement being for brass rather than strings. A down scale glissando with Nick's voice in a slightly higher register than usual. A cha cha with bossa nova overtones, plus touches of Herb Alpert's Tijuana Brass. Nick reveals his problem with communication, it is so much easier to communicate in the lyrics of a song. The first three verses also indicate the desire to be a recluse, there is a safety and escapism to be found amongst books and records. The Fairport Convention trio of Richard Thompson, Dave Mattacks, and Dave Pegg are also present on this track. The last three verses consist of six lines rather than the two of the first three verses, again perhaps Nick juxtaposed two poems, it is only the second half that concerns Hazy Jane. Here the protagonist of the lyrics is more bewildered than critical of his inability to mix with the crowds.

AT THE CHIME OF A CITY CLOCK, introduces Mike Kowalski on drums and some excellent alto saxophone from Ray Warleigh introduces a city jazz club's atmosphere. This is a song of ambivalence, the desire to be with people but then feeling ill at ease within the group. The initial verses present the fun of a city, then suddenly as though someone has struck a bell the desire for solitude returns. This desire for seclusion is considered abnormal by persons who do not understand. How can a person who has never experienced depression understand the many facets, the sudden changes, at times as happy as a clown, that is until the clown falls down. This recording is definitive one can't imagine it being improved. The joy of 'riding the range of a London Street', the listener might imagine Astrud Gilberto singing this lovely song.

ONE OF THESE THINGS FIRST, a jazz waltz, John Wood's recording fills the whole stereo with acoustic sounds, yet it only comprises of a quartet of piano, bass, drums and guitar. A song for all the opportunities available at the out-set of life. Although the lyric presents so many ideas of what he could have been, he never informs us just what he is now. He does say that he could have been her statue or friend, but the inference is that he would help her rather than just stand and ignore her. In Nick's melancholy and meditative state he would sit like a statue for hours.

HAZEY JANE I, she is slow things move too fast for her. She is an under-achiever, yet full of imagination, living a lie, or is she? Nick is talking to Jane of himself, all the questions are rhetorical, he is asking if she shares his emotions. This is a self denigration song, searching for new ways to solve a problem. Nick turns the lyric on its head in the last verse, he talks to Jane of

84

her new man and how confusing everything is, but it is Nick who feels that he is living a lie.

BRYTER LAYTER, an instrumental interlude, the un-named flute player plays a nice melody that deserves a lyric. I have another idea for the title of this album and track. When typing some words I often strike two keys simultaneously, R,T,and Y are all next to each other, so many times I have typed 'Bryt' in error, maybe just maybe Nick did the same, perhaps it wasn't the weather forecast after all. I would suspect that most Drake-followers will be thinking, Nick Drake wrote all his lyrics by hand, he probably did.

FLY, is the first track to include ex-Velvet Underground stalwart, welshman John Cale. Nick is nearer to the microphone than usual as he almost recites the words before singing in a key that is considerably uncomfortable for him. Cale's harpsichord is hidden somewhere behind the sound of Nick's guitar, the viola I find unnecessarily intrusive. The imploring for a second chance, the necessity to talk over the problem together. I wonder if the last verse lyric should read 'See' rather than 'Sea', although without the prefix 'then', neither of the words really sit with the thoughts of the lyric. Eminent Drake researcher Frank Kornelussen refers to the protagonist as part of the tragedy, perhaps he is correct, the lyric can be observed from various directions. This one is for you dear reader, what do you think was in Nick Drake's mind ?

POOR BOY includes Chris McGregor on piano, apparently he was stoned-out on ganja at the time, it certainly is not evident in his keyboard playing, he plays expertly here. A jazz, bossa nova, shuffle, this is 'Nick Drake sings soul music'. Backing vocalists Doris Troy and Pat Arnold are added to augment the alto saxophone of Ray Warleigh and the earlier mentioned piano. The girl singers are given the chorus to themselves, the song is composed using descending chords in a manner used for the earlier song 'The Man in the Shed'. Surely someone at Island Records must have thought that this track might have potential as a single release. This is self parody, this is Nick Drake feeling that he should suffer for his art, forgetting his roots and kind upbringing and pretending to be poor due to 'throwing his coins over his shoulder'. He mentions his desire for a wife, his concern for his health, his never helping his neighbour, he is poor indeed. A man who has decided that he should suffer for his art.

NORTHERN SKY, with John Cale playing piano with one hand only on the top half of the keyboard. A gentle shuffling rhythm for a song of optimism, whoever 'she' is in the lyric she certainly has improved Nick's outlook. She has brightened his sky, the sun never shines from the north in Britain anyway. He is concerned that she really wants him for his brains and not for his money, but he had little money at the time he was barely scraping an existence. Once more death rears its ugly head with the line 'Would you love me 'til I'm dead', alternatively this line may mean 'Will you love me forever'. All the emotions that he has desired are suddenly nearer, he almost has emotion in the palm of his hand.

SUNDAY, is an instrumental to close a truly magnificent album. The exquisite flute playing really deserves to be recognised on these later album re-releases. This is Nick Drakes answer to the song 'Elizabethan Serenade' it has all the hallmarks of that olde folk music style.

John Cale's involvement came after he heard Nick's first album he requested Nick's address from Joe Boyd. Cale visited Nick and together they returned to the studio and added over-dubs to the two tracks detailed earlier. In an effort to lighten Nick's depressed sate of mind Joe Boyd also arranged for a few evenings out. They played cards with a cockney friend of Joe's, Joe felt that this chap was particularly therapeutic for Nick, he may have inadvertently found a partial solution to Nick's problem. The cockney friend (name not known) would ignore Nick's lack of response to questions and force tea and food on him, he just generally jollied him along. Nick responded with smiles, he did not have to converse the man made Nick's mind up for him. A sort of 'cruel to be kind' bullying, organising him telling him by answering his own questions in the affirmative, discouraging the mood rather than tolerating it.

The 'Bryter Layter' album is difficult to fault, Joe Boyd maintains that it is the only album that he produced that he with which he was totally satisfied. However Boyd was becoming increasingly frustrated with the groups and solo artists under his control. The Incredible String Band wanted to record a double thematic album entitled 'U'. Sandy Denny the now ex-Fairport Convention singer did not wish to go solo against Boyd's advice, she had formed the group Fotheringay, and he was also at logger-heads at times with the talented Richard Thompson. The stress was tremendous and Joe Boyd decided to sell Witchseason to Island. He was offered a less strenuous job at Warner Brothers Records in Los Angeles and he accepted. As part of the sale of Witchseason to Island Joe Boyd insisted that special care should be taken of Nick Drake.

'Bryter Layter' sold 15,000 copies which was three times better than the first album but still pretty poor in comparison with other artists such as Fairport Convention, their 'Liege and Lief' album (their fourth album) had become an international hit selling more than 200,000 copies. The poor sales were obviously a disappointment to both Nick and Joe Boyd, it was only a few weeks later that Nick advised Joe Boyd that the next album would be acoustic without embellishment.

During March 1970 Nick toured with Sandy Denny's group Fotheringay. He played at Birmingham, Leicester, Manchester, Bristol and finally at The Royal Festival Hall once more on March 30th. He also joined the bill of Spencer Davis and Graham Bond at Bedford College during early May. It was around this time that Nick played some Saturday's at 'Cousins Club' in London's Greek Street. On 25th June Nick supported Ralph McTell at a show at Ewell Technical College, this is believed to be Nick's last ever live show performance. According to Ralph McTell, Nick never completed this performance, during the song 'Fruit Tree' he just stood up and walked off stage.

Joe Boyd's return to the United States was traumatic for Nick, he had lost his mentor and friend in one foul swoop. Nick decided to return home to his parents in Tanworth-in-Arden. The loving parents noticed immediately that there had been a change in their son, his introversion had become intense, his lack of communication now had spread to talking to his parents. An extremely concerned Rodney Drake telephoned Joe Boyd in Los Angeles and asked for his assistance. Joe spoke to Nick and explained that it was not an embarrassment to request psychiatric help, most americans had a psychiatrist as well as a doctor. Nick understanding Joe Boyd's care and concern visited his local doctor who prescribed anti-depressant tablets. These it was subsequently agreed were incorrect for Nick's problem, they created even more shifts in behaviour. Nick would regularly stop taking the tablets in an effort to 'see the situation through' with his own strength of character, sadly withdrawal from the drug sent him even deeper into despondency.

Molly and Rodney gave Nick as much help as any parents could be expected to give, they doted on their son and wanted him to be well. Nick eventually became more morose and sat for hours in contemplation just looking out of the window or at his own feet. The Island Record Label owner at the time was Chris Blackwell, a man who cared deeply for quality music. He was aware of the codicil on the agreement with Joe Boyd, he decided that Nick Drake might wish to take a holiday in his Villa in Spain. Nick accepted and it seemed to put Nick into some form of remission from his melancholy, he returned from Spain ready to record his third album.

87

THE INFLUENCES

This music crept by me on the waters,
Allaying both their fury and my passion
With its sweet air
William Shakespeare (1564-1616)

JACKSON C. FRANK.

Born Buffalo New York in 1943, his family moved to Cheektowago New York in 1954 when Jackson was eleven. He wanted to be in show business, he would learn songs to sing for his family and friends. His life consisted of one long series of bad luck the first was the most traumatic. During school lessons the school caught fire and eighteen of his friends were killed. Jackson escaped but was severely injured, he suffered burns over 80% of his body. Burns are extremely difficult to treat, Jackson spent most of his teen years either in hospital or returning as an out-patient for grafts and medication.

Whilst in hospital he learned to play guitar, he also commenced writing his own songs. He wanted to learn songs from the american civil war and his parents took him to Memphis where by chance he met Elvis Presley. He also met and befriended John Kay a struggling musician who would be a success after he formed the group Steppenwolf. Josh White, Sonny Terry and Brownie McGhee were influences on Jackson's early work. Jackson also went to Gerde's Nightclub where he saw newcomer Bob Dylan. It was after seeing Bob Dylan that Jackson decided that he could do better.

Finally the insurance paid him for the school fire that almost killed him. He lived with the pain of the burn tissue by regularly taking pain killer tablets. He was attending college learning english and journalism but decided that he would prefer to be a singer songwriter. He decided to try his luck in England and travelled by cruise liner to Southampton. On this Atlantic journey he wrote one of his most famous songs 'Blues Run the Game', the song concerns fate and how it should be cast to the wind.

Once in London he decided to try to get club work. He was different to all the performers at the time, he insisted on wearing three piece suits, most of the suits were pin-stripped. So looking like an estate agent he would play on the stage in sweaty night clubs but looking the coolest person present. He could be seen walking around London in his pin-stripped suit plus a bowler hat, only the traditional jazz band's of the time wore bowler hats, Acker Bilk and Chris Charlesworth with his City Gents to name just two.

In 1965 Jackson met Paul Simon who was also living in London and for a while shared and apartment with him. Paul Simon was so impressed with Jackson's songs that he produced his first album putting up his own personal money for the venture. It was at these recording sessions that Paul Simon learned that Jackson had a serious problem, stage-fright. He was so nervous in the studio that he sat out of sight behind a series of screens. They were unsure if he was nervous or was doing this to protect his special guitar tuning. The recording was so difficult that the engineer and Paul Simon convinced Jackson to play and sing so that they could set up the volume levels. These sound checks ultimately became the tracks used on the album, Jackson had no idea that they were recording and consequently gave a reasonable performance. The complete album was recorded in three hours, Al Stewart an up and coming guitarist/singer played guitar back-up on the track 'Yellow Walls'.

Jackson's stage-fright got so bad he couldn't play live. He was living at the time with Sandy Denny who was later to sing lead for The Strawberry Hill Boys (Strawbs), Fairport Convention, Fotheringay, and then went solo before her untimely death. She included three of Jackson's songs on her first solo album. The album was so popular in London, John Peel could not stop playing the tracks on his radio programme, Nightride. Jackson played 'Blues Run the Game', 'Jimmy Clay', 'Just Like Anything', 'Carnival', 'You Never Wanted Me', live on Nightride on 9th October 1968.

He had been living in London for three years, his stage-fight meant that he rarely worked, living on his diminishing insurance funds. He also suffered terrible bouts of depression, he finally decided to return to America settling in Woodstock, New York early 1969. He gave up the music business, he suffered from song-writer's block, he took a job as a journalist. Life was better for a while he had a son and family life stopped his deep mental depression.

Fate intervened, his son died of acute cystic fibrosis, his wife left him. The depression returned, the anti-depressant tablets reacted against the analgesic medication for the burn pains. He developed a thyroid problem which made him gain wait until he was considerably obese. This chain of events culminated with him experiencing a nervous breakdown. He suffered migraines and heard voices in his head, causing him to be introverted and un-communicative. He hospitalised himself but found that the doctors had decided that he was mentally ill, he escaped from the pills and unconventional treatments.

He lived on the streets, certain that 'they' were searching for him. He spent almost 20 years living as a derelict, staying in doss houses and poor shelters.

He was taking a multitude of pills most he had no idea of their nature, pills for pills sake, if they seemed to help then take another. He decided to return to hospital, more pills which did not improve his demeanour, introverted and un-communicative once more. To add to the problems of the burns he now had arthritis in his legs which meant that he needed a stick to walk. and then only slowly. Whilst sitting on a house stoop a gang of youths that were travelling the neighbourhood shooting derelicts and crazy-men found Jackson. They shot him in the left eye with an air gun blinding him.

By chance Jim Abbott recognised Jackson on the street one day, he gave him an apartment in which to live and assisted him with food and clothes. Abbott also found a considerate and sympathetic doctor who at last diagnosed Jackson's mental problem correctly. He was not a paranoid schizophrenic after all. So after 20 years on the run from himself Jackson was back on an even keel. He was provided with a guitar and started playing again. It was 1996, he was calling himself Jack Frank, so far he has not recorded an album, we wait.

WILLIAM BLAKE (1757-1827)

William Blake was born in London his father an Irishman. William was an extremely obstinate child and refused to attend school, he was educated by his mother. A modern family with few restraints, Blake although extremely stubborn was an extremely happy child who loved his parents. Whilst out walking Blake had a religious experience, he claimed that he saw visions of angels in a tree in Peckham London. He was extremely intelligent, and his father could not understand why he would pretend to see this vision, and almost resorted to punishing him with a thrashing.

Blake read all the classical writers, Shakespeare, Milton, Ben Jonson, and of course the Bible which became his predominant influence. In his education he taught himself Hebrew, Greek, Latin, Italian and French, mostly before he reached the age of 14. Blake became an apprenticed engraver, and selected James Basire to be his tutor. Blake was so accomplished with a pencil he was able to choose his employer. Strangely he refused an apprenticeship from William Ryland, his reason was that Ryland had the mark of the gallows around him, twelve months later Ryland was hanged for committing forgery.

He remained with James Basire for seven happy years. After receiving his indentures he moved to The Royal Academy at Somerset House. He was studying gothic art and the nude form. He married Catherine Boucher the illiterate daughter of a gardener in 1782, and his new neighbours were surgeon Joshua Reynolds, anatomist John Hunter, and Jane Hogarth the widow of the artist. Blake also increased his interest in poetry, previously it was just an amusing pastime. Blake's poems were first published in 1783, one written when Blake was only twelve years old. The poems were almost discarded as superfluous by Blake, but he was tired of the traditionalism of The Royal Academy. Encouraged by his friends he commenced writing, his first work 'Island of the Moon' a satire was not completed and remained unknown until the 20th century.

'Songs of Innocence and of Experience' (1789), with the contrary sides of the soul presented in short poems was published. He also loved aphorisms (an aphorism must convince the reader that it is either universally true, or true of every member of the class that it refers), some which Blake wrote may be pertinent to Nick Drake. 'I sometimes try to be miserable so that I may do more work'. 'The apple tree never asks the beech how he shall grow, nor the lion the horse, how he shall take his prey'.'He who pretends to be either painter or engraver without being a master of drawing is an imposter.'

Blake observed that 'Cruelty has a human heart, and jealousy a human face'. Blake's principal prose work was 'The Marriage of Heaven and Hell' (1793), he was becoming a revolutionary philosopher. 'Without contraries there is no progression', he wrote. In 'Marriage' 'Good' is passive and obeys reason, and is therefore Heaven, 'Evil' is the active springing from energy and therefore Hell. Many of Blake's outlooks on heaven and hell coincided with those of Nick Drake. Blake moved to Lambeth in 1793, and resumed engraving, he drew scenes from his latest book, to expound his principles, and presented the errors of the morals of the day. His engraving was a new form of painted illumination, and looked beautiful on the printed page. He was renounced and criticised and never achieved affluence, he was also cheated on commission payments.

At his death he left no debts but was buried in an unmarked grave in Bunhill Fields Cemetery. Catherine outlived him by four years but eventually died of a broken heart, she just wanted to rejoin her William.

Blake was influenced himself by Milton and Shakespeare, Wordsworth was in turn influenced by Blake. Blake questioned the significance and merit of all things artistic. He investigated through his writing poetry, religion, philosophy, art, and perhaps was too vehement in his condemnations of a society that would have supported him, that is if he had been more condescending in their favour. Blake's complete writings were collected by Geoffrey Keynes in 1925 and their availability today makes for stimulating reading.

ARTHUR RIMBAUD (1854-1891)

A strict mother and an Army Captain for a father, meant that his childhood was filled with discipline. Arthur had two devoted sisters Vitalie and Isabelle. Father left home for an another woman when Arthur was six years old. Whilst studying at Charleville a teacher George Izambard suggested that he read the work of Victor Hugo. Arthur's first published work was a poem in 1870 which won a prize at the Concorde Academique.

Tired of schooling Arthur ran away to Paris and became a beatnik, due to his frugal existence he found himself homosexually abused. He met Charles Bretagne who introduced Rimbaud to occult magic, and also to the work of Paul Verlaine and Baudelaire. Rimbaud met and liked Verlaine, in fact Verlaine left his wife to live with Rimbaud.

The scandal that followed meant that they decided to leave France and they set up home as lovers in Soho London, it was 1872. The relationship became more difficult as Rimbaud travelled to France and Belgium, leaving and returning to Verlaine many times. Exasperated with the relationship Verlaine shot Rimbaud in the hand after a lover's tiff, and was sentenced to two years hard labour.

The writing of Rimbaud was embargoed due to the infamous relationship, Rimbaud set aside all his writings and never wrote again, it was 1873. On release from prison Verlaine (still in love with Rimbaud) and Arthur met, argued and never saw each other again. Rimbaud travelled to Cyprus, caught typhoid, returned to France to recuperate. In he 1880 travelled to Aden, Ethiopia, and other parts of Africa. He was a vagabond involved in gun-running and was seen as an adventurer and a mercenary.

Now back in France Verlaine assumed that Rimbaud was missing presumed dead and wrote of Arthur in his poems, Verlaine's work was lauded and his fame grew. Verlaine then collected Rimbaud's work and published it as 'Illuminations' which is recognised as Rimbaud's greatest work. The response to Rimbaud's work was astounding, he immediately became the darling idol of the avant garde, although they assumed he was dead.

Rimbaud totally unaware of his new fame was in Aden and found he had a tumour in his right knee. He returned home to France and lived with devoted sister Isabelle. The tumour was deemed cancer and Rimbaud's right leg was amputated. The awareness that the prodigal had returned was short lived by the Paris Society, as Rimbaud suddenly died of complications from the cancer, he was 37 years old.

WILLIAM BUTLER YEATS, (1865-1939)

An enigma, a man who wrote his best work whilst in old age. Born near Dublin of an artistic family. In his early work he was a romantic, with regular escapes into The Irish Fairyland. He wrote 'The Rose' 'The Wind among the Reeds', and a long narrative poem 'The Wandering of Oisin'. The latter was the extended tale of Oisin and St Patrick and Oisin's travels for 300 years.

Yeats and Lady Gregory founded the Irish Literary Theatre, which later became the Abbey theatre. Yeats decided to write plays for the theatre and 'Land of Hearts Desire' was the first in 1894, a fairy story. 'Deirdre' (1907) is the legendary gaelic tale which John Millington Synge retold as 'Deidre of the Sorrows' in 1909. It is the story of old King Conchubar, and Deidre the beautiful child he found reared and married. She runs away with Naisi. The King pretends to forgive them and traps them into returning to the castle. Naisi is murdered and Deirdre stabs herself. Yeats mysticism and his love of all things magic is manifest in 'Ideas of Good and Evil'(1903) , which was included in some editions of 'The Tower'. 'A Vision' (1925) was more esoteric the psyche was shown in various forms set between points of demarcation, and how the soul would be transformed between this life and the life after death. Yeats also used other gaelic characters in his work such as Cuchulainn, Fergus, Emer, all part of his 'Elaborate Vision'.

Yeats grew tired of his early work and in 1914 moved into what is known as his mature phase with the aptly named 'Responsibilities'. However it was subtitled 'In dreams become responsibilities'. 'The Tower' became his best known work as it became a standard for in-school teaching. 'Sailing to Byzantium' taken from 'The Tower', describes how the soul can sing louder once the source of wisdom is located. 'Among School Children' also from 'The Tower' presents an old scarecrow of a man returning to a convent school, here he remembers a lover from his past and imagines her as one of these school children.

Yeats also presented his auto-biography in three parts between 1916 and 1936, published in one volume in 1938. He apparently became a member of the Irish Republican Brotherhood, somewhat unusual for a protestant. He stated that his heart was with all Ireland with no favour for either side.

MOSE ALLISON

born 1927 in Mississippi, influenced by the blues learned to play piano and formed a jazz trio. His first release 'Black Country Suite' in 1957 was hailed as a masterpiece. Also influenced Georgie Fame (and others) as is obvious when listening to his 'Best of' release on compact disc.

ALBERT CAMUS (1913-60)

a French novelist who seems to have influenced a great many intellectuals but receives very little acknowledgement. Camus was born and educated in Algeria and during the second world war was a member of the French Resistance movement. His first novel 'L'Etranger' was influenced by Jean Paul Sartre and his existentialist outlook on life. Camus and Sartre joined forces after the war establishing the left wing 'Paris Daily Combat' newspaper. The honeymoon with Sartre lasted a short while, they argued over political direction and parted company, Camus abandoned political activities completely. Amongst others Camus wrote 'La Piste' (1947), and the play 'Caligula' (1948), Camus was awarded the Nobel prize for literature in 1957. Although Leonard Cohen was acknowledged to have read Camus the influences are few and far between.

BOB DYLAN

born Robert Allen Zimmerman 24th May 1941. Recognised predominantly for his early songs and lyrics. Quoted by Allen Ginsberg as being the greatest poet of the 20th century, few scholars will argue after reading and hearing his early work prior to his motor-cycle accident. Bob Dylan has influenced all the singer songwriters since he released his first album. He suffered from 'writer's block' for some years, he did return to form later with the album 'Blood on the Tracks' in 1975 but it is chiefly his work before 1968 which derives most of the accolades. Dylan also wrote the novel 'Tarantula' in the 'stream of consciousness' style and also has gained acceptance as a painter

SONNY TERRY & BROWNIE McGHEE

They were the longest lasting and most celebrated partnership in the history of blues music. Sonny Terry played harmonica and Brownie McGhee guitar. They first worked together in 1939 when they were both in their twenties, Sonny Terry died in 1986. They were together for most of the time, they did have plenty of arguments, on the assumption that only fools never disagree this was likely during the 47 years of partnership. Sonny Terry was blinded early in life and also had the complications of suffering polio, his disability never prevented him from pursuing his musical career. He had recorded with Blind Boy Fuller before teaming up with McGhee, Terry also worked occasionally with Brownie's brother Sticks McGhee. They became very popular with white audiences playing numerous folk, jazz and blues festivals, Terry's vamping style of harmonica, coupled with vocal whoops and interjections, against Brownie's rhythmic guitaring and flexible voice.

94

BERT JANSCH

Born Herbert Jansch in Glasgow in 1943. Learned guitar whilst living in Edinburgh, his father had left the home and never returned. An introvert, a loner, preferring a solitary existence. Decided that his best method of communication would be through music. He lived in a succession of houses and flats with Robin Williamson and Clive Palmer (later Incredible String Band). He tried piano lessons and hated it, took a job as a gardener and bought a guitar with his earnings. Listened to Brownie McGhee, Leadbelly, and Woody Guthrie. He travelled through France and down to Morocco, and to Tangiers. He called this his 'Kerouac' period. Bert married a girl named Linda (surname forgotten) to get a travel visa. (They divorced and he re-married Heather Sewell in 1968). He is reputed that he learned to master the guitar in three months. He listened and learned from virtuoso of the guitar Davy Graham, everyone did. Living in Camden Town he was almost penniless and was playing a borrowed guitar and singing into a tape recorder in his kitchen. This was the scene where Bert was to make his first album. The album was an immediate success but Bert saw little of the royalties from it or for his compositions, he sold the lot for £100. Jansch was the prototype for many up and coming guitarist songwriters. He released albums at regular intervals became Transatlantic Records top seller in the U.K. He joined Pentangle in 1967 and with Danny Thompson, Jacquie McShee, John Renbourn and Terry Cox, and the group went International.

JOSH WHITE, (1908-1969) came originally from Mississippi, became accepted on the cabaret circuit in New York. This was years before the blues revival, he was extremely left wing, his songs were anti-establishment but as he was black the McCarthy investigators considered his views unimportant. His son was also named Josh White and was born in 1940, he too sang and composed, but it was his father that was the bluesman who had paid his dues. He was never really fully accepted back into the blues boom of the 60s but he recorded many albums usually under the name of Joshua White.

PINK MOON (Island Records ILPS 9184, 1972)

The music in my heart I bore,
Long after it was heard no more.
William Wordsworth (1770-1850)

Nick contacted John Wood at Sound Techniques and asked if he could record some new tracks. For a few days had Nick rented a flat in Muswell Hill, London. Nick arrived at the studio with his guitar and in two evening sessions recorded eleven songs. The tracks are all first takes except for one 'Pink Moon' which has a piano over-dub. When they were completed and played back John Wood asked what Nick wanted them to sound like in their completed form. He was astonished to learn that the tracks should be released exactly as recorded, no frills, no orchestra, nothing. John was also surprised that the completed eleven songs lasted less than 30 minutes which would make for a very short album. The recorded acoustic guitar sound produced by John Wood for the album is marvellous, a credit to his solo engineering.

PINK MOON, has Nick playing piano and guitar. Many Drake followers consider that a 'Pink Moon' is a euphemism for death. In the early parts of the song Nick is actually singing 'Pinka Moon'. Taking the death scenario one step further he intimates that it is on its way and will get us all, as death is the one inevitability then it may just be the inference that Nick had intended for himself.

PLACE TO BE, has a lyric resemblance to The Beatles 'Help' in the first line. In fact the complete lyric fits perfectly into the melody of that song, try it. I would think that melody just might have been in Nick's head as he wrote the lyrics. It is another call for help, 'he is weaker than the palest blue', 'greener than the hill', yet he has grown 'darker than the deepest sea'. Nick recognising the changes that have taken place over the years, now he needs real help, the last line cries out 'So weak in this need for you'.

ROAD presents us with his quest for survival. Nick sounds like Donovan here and the song is also similar to Donovan's 'Ricki Tiki Tavi' from the album 'Open Road' released in 1970. Nick is at the crossroads not knowing which way to turn. He convinces himself that he can see his way through his problems, or is he anticipating a journey to the stars, the 'moon' looms large within the song once again.

WHICH WILL, another song with a Beatles influence. Another song which presents a long series of un-answered questions. Some reviewers have suggested that this is a song for someone jilted and rejected, surely he is just asking 'which' rather than 'who'. The answers are not evident, if he is rejected by her then there is no decision in the lyrics, he continues to ask 'which will you love the best' at the last line, in the penultimate line he insists that she decide now. She does suggest however that she might not take him.

HORN, dextrous solo guitar picking, a short interval leads into....

...THINGS BEHIND THE SUN. The song that cries out for a Robert Kirby arrangement, he could even add one now. Nick seems to be suffering from the problems of people who stare. This is probably Nick's most carefully constructed poem, it is extremely accomplished it is ideal for an in-depth scrutiny without the music. The rain returns, it certainly has become an anathema to Nick over the years. The lyric has the elements of a person experiencing severe mental turmoil, the warnings, reaching the depths, the ground is as low as it is possible to go. If rain is for the depressions then flying is for the better times when everything is improving and the sun is shining. The movement in your brain sends you out into the rain. A man bares his soul to us and nobody is listening, they say it has all been said. Absolutely sublime Nick Drake, but the likelihood is that a happy man would not be able to provide such an honest and sombre warning, to himself.

KNOW, a song of just four lines, 18 words of which only four are not repeated. These four words are important, 'love', 'Care', 'not there'. The first two lines are contradictory and the second pair suggest that he is hiding from her. So much gleaned from so little. A blues to which Nick hums a short introduction and repeats the guitar riff. It was suggested that this is his suicide note, my thoughts are that it is a child's game played by an adult. This track was later used by Nike running shoes in their advertisements. As Nick was once a champion runner I would suspect he would give a wry smile at the thought.

PARASITE, returns us to the city. Travelling on the Northern Line underground trains, everyone looks down (or at the overhead adverts), rather than stare at the person sitting opposite. This is not just Nick looking down at his shoes in contemplation this is everyone on the train. Over hearing conversations is inevitable when people are packed so close together. The chime from the city clock returns, although this time 'not' hearing the bell from the steeple tall. Born with a silver spoon in his mouth Nick is now making his way without money, his own way. To survive he has to borrow, this instills in his mind that he has become a parasite. Strangely on this song Nick makes his only grammatical error, probably due to americanisms or in the cause of rhyming. People who are executed by the rope are 'hanged' not 'hung', but Nick may of course used this word to complete the rhyme with 'fun'.

97

FREE RIDE is titled 'RIDE' on the liner notes but 'Free Ride' on the lyric sheet. A continuation of the concern that he is becoming a parasite. This has been referred to as paranoia but that is far too heartfelt, he needs financial assistance, if they are so rich why can't they help, but who are 'They'.

HARVEST BREED, is the second extremely short lyric, this time just five lines. This is Nick reaching the depths of depression, falling fast and free. What is the harvest breed, this song has the feel of 'Helter Skelter' which was The Beatles method of falling fast and free. Is it preparing to be part of one's environment or as one reviewer remarked, is it anticipating the end ?

FROM THE MORNING, up-beat, the final track is an optimistic song of a new day dawning. She flits around like a butterfly, she is ubiquitous, she plays her games in the morning sun. A surprisingly light and energetic song that ends such a deep and somewhat oppressive album, not all the tracks betray doom and gloom but in hindsight it is difficult to see much brightness.

A few days later Nick arrived at the offices of Island Records. Dave Sandison (Island Records Press Officer) saw him waiting in reception and invited him up to his office for a coffee, which Nick accepted. Nick was carrying a tape reel box under his arm, they spoke for a while although it was far from a conversation and Nick then made his excuses and left, still carrying the tape box. A while later Sandison had a call from the reception desk saying that Nick Drake had left a tape box on the desk. This proved to be the master recording tape of The Pink Moon album. Dave Sandison arranged for a copy to be made for safety purposes, and the art work was requested from artist Michael Trevithick. This art work was later found by Sandison in a pile of debris in an unused office, he asked if he could have it and took it home. Years later after Nick's death he presented it to Molly Drake and it can be seen in photographs of her home hanging on the wall, an extremely nice and generous gesture. Some of the cover photographs of Nick were taken around Hampstead Heath by Keith Morris. Gabrielle Drake would later remark that the photograph of Nick sitting on a park bench looking at the ground captured the exact character and mood of her brother.

Once more a Nick Drake album was a commercial disaster, it sent Nick into an even deeper despairing depression. It was apparent that he wanted his work to be heard and accepted by the masses, yet it was so eclectic that it was aimed at intellectual listeners. Molly and Rodney Drake were again concerned although this time even more than on previous occasions. In April 12th 1972 Nick Drake was diagnosed as having a complete nervous breakdown. He was moving in short time spans from elation to despair.

Nick decided that perhaps his chances of becoming a famous singer songwriter were slight so he decided to take alternative employment. It is alleged that he visited an army recruitment centre but decided against joining. This idea might seem unusual for an individual of such gentleness and intellect, but the army does not ask questions they give orders and arrange the person's life completely, Nick would not need to make any decisions, the communication would be coming in one direction, directly at him.

He went for an interview to become a trainee computer programmer, or perhaps salesman. He was surprised when they offered him the position. After a week of basic training he was sent by the company to work in London, this was a mistake on their part he resigned after a few days and returned home to his parents. Nick spent a few weeks in hospital for mental checks but apart from tablets there seemed to be nothing else they could do for him. The tablets that were prescribed were tryptizol, the family and Tim it is alleged were not advised on the safety of the drug. Molly and Rodney always worried for Nick's state of mind had locked away all the other drugs, they had no worries over tryptizol, after all it was prescribed for a particular purpose, namely deep nervous depression.

In February 1974 Nick again called John Wood and said he had some tracks to record. Joe Boyd was in England at the time and was present when Nick recorded 'Rider on the Wheel', 'Hanging on a Star', Voice from the Mountain' and 'Black Eyed Dog'. These would subsequently be added to the posthumous album release 'Time of No reply'. 'Black Eyed Dog' was the last commercially recorded song by Nick, it mentions 'Death's head stalking his door'. These recording were not completed in the normal manner, Nick had lost the art of singing and playing simultaneously, so each was recorded with Nick's vocal over-dubbed.

Francoise Hardy the French singer expressed some interest in Nick's recordings and Nick went to France to meet her. He lived on a barge for a while, it has not been revealed if any relationship between the two developed but he did visit with a her on at least three occasions. Nick had a girl friend at the time, they visited Paris together. Nick was attempting to learn some conversational French by using his mother's Linguaphone record and book course.

When Nick returned from France he presented to his mother as a gift 'Le Mythe de Sysyphe' a book by Albert Camus. The myth of sisyphus is a book that discusses the contemplation of suicide, it presents the existentialist argument for the ultimate act of taking one's own life. The world around is absurd so the only way for freedom is in death, a statement of which Jean Paul Sartre is in agreement in his work. Molly read the book wondering if this

99

was deemed as a message from Nick, but she was never to know. Nick had relaxed in his normal habits of hygiene. Friends who saw him said that he had grown his fingernails to an extraordinary lengths, he also rarely washed and had almost stopped eating.

Molly said that Nick wanted to suffer for his art, he wanted to dispense with material possessions. He wanted to communicate and was totally frustrated by his inability to reach the listeners with his message. He did not wish to live at home but could not bear to be away. A man with a domestic ambivalence that caused him such despair. The family gave him their love and devotion which Nick certainly appreciated, he returned it when ever he was in a fit state of mind

On November 25th 1974 Molly heard Nick moving around in the night. He was an insomniac and preferred to write his songs in the early hours of the morning. Often Nick would come down stairs to the kitchen and prepare himself some corn-flakes. It was regular occurrence and usually Molly would get up and go down and chat with him whilst he ate. On this particular night she did not. Rodney Drake said that she never heard him, but one interview stated that she just fell immediately back to sleep after hearing him. The next morning she allowed Nick to sleep in, he often would do this as he was late going to bed. She thought it was time that he was awake and went to his room only to find Nick dead on his bed.

The coroner after hearing the evidence deemed the death as suicide, Nick Drake was 26 years of age. He had taken an over dose of tryptizol but Molly is convinced that he had no idea that an overdose of the drug was dangerous.

At the funeral it was surprising that many of the friends that attended did not know each other. Nick had managed to maintain a separation between these people, it was as though he had kept his music and personal worlds separate. Nick Drake was buried at St Mary Magdalene Graveyard, Tanworth-in Arden, the gravestone is inscribed.....'Remembered with Love'.

The Drake family donated money to the church to maintain the condition of the organ and a small plaque is attached to the organ remembering Nick Drake. He will never grow old he will always be that handsome young man wrapped in a blanket, smiling at the camera as if he did not have a care in the world.

TIME OF NO REPLY (Hannibal HNBX 5302, 1986)

Hardly does a composer appear :
than people start devoting essays to him,
and weighing his music down with ambitious definitions.
They do far greater harm than the fiercest detractor could do.

Claude Debussy (1862-1918)

So much was written about Nick Drake after his sudden demise. Re-evaluations of his work abounded, reviewers who criticised now re-listened and enthused, if only it had happened a few years earlier. The first album title of 'Five Leaves Left' was in fact an omen, one leaf for each year in Nick's remaining life.

All three albums were released in a boxed set the original covers were changed to be top opening slip cases. This was followed by the release of the three albums plus a fourth album which when it was released separately became 'The Time of No Reply' album. In the U.S.A., a collection was released entitled 'Nick Drake', it consisted of tracks taken from the first two albums. In the U.K. 'Heaven in a Wild Flower' was released containing 14 previously released tracks. When Island Records decided to delete Nick's albums they were retained by Hannibal Records another of Joe Boyd's enterprises, Nick's entire output is now leased to Rykodisc.

The clamour for all the other recordings resulted in the album 'Time of no Reply' which consisted of six tracks from the 'Five Leaves Left' sessions (1968), the four last recorded tracks (1974) which were the start of a new album, and three home demonstration songs. The cover notes states ten previously un-released songs, seven completely new songs, plus the four 'Last session' tracks.

TIME OF NO REPLY (1968), a song for a person who has all the answers, it is unnecessary to respond. Hello and Goodbye are mentioned the title of the Tim Buckley's album that so impressed Nick at the time. If nature does not need to reply then why should he.

I WAS MADE TO LOVE MAGIC (1968), is the track arranged by Richard Hewson which once recorded was discarded by Nick. The arrangement makes Nick sound like pianist singer Peter Skellern the arrangement would be ideally suited to Skellern. The arrangement has a baroque charm, it is obvious why this song was chosen by Richard Hewson it contains a superb melody line. I have listened to the arrangement of this track many times, sure it does sound ordinary but it is far from poor, Richard Hewson should not have been so inconsiderately discarded. Robert Kirby's arrangements are more conducive to presenting Nick's work perfectly but here Hewson succeeds admirably.

JOEY (1968) an ode to lost youth, an out-take with a different studio sound, possibly the microphones were situated differently. Joey is a woman, or is she a cat or dog, we never really find out.

CLOTHES OF SAND (1968) have covered your face, given you meaning but taken my place. A deep and involved lyric, has she become a muslim and now must cover her face? The sand could present the sands of Arabia, home of Islam, or might that just be Morocco where Nick travelled. Is she now locked away in solitude where she has changed her name, if not then something very powerful has become between her and him.

MAN IN A SHED (1968), an acoustic solo version of the previously released song. Nick manages in nearly all his recordings to play and sing the songs identically.

MAYFAIR (1968) was also recorded by Millie Small the black singer of 'My Boy Lollipop' fame. The song was allegedly written for Molly Drake. Nick is referring to the exclusively rich full of fame and lacking love, sounds a perfect description. The melody is played to sound like John Sebastian of The Lovin' Spoonful, the tune is reminiscent of The Kink's 'Sunny Afternoon', which is a song that may have been used before as the basis of a melody by Nick. The song is so instant and catchy I can not understand why it was remaindered from either of the first two albums.

FLY (1969), is taken from Nick's home recording session, the compact disc booklet seems to infer that Nick lived in Tamworth, rather than Tanworth-in-Arden. To these ears the song is so much better without John Cale's viola. Nick is recording this at home why did he try to sing it in such a painful key signature?

THE THOUGHTS OF MARY JANE (1968), includes Richard Thompson on electric guitar. This is so similar to the work being recorded at the time by Tim Buckley. Thompson plays with the same refinement Lee Underwood was providing for Tim. This track would have been perfect for inclusion on Tim Buckley's 'Blue Afternoon' album.

BEEN SMOKING TOO LONG (1967/8), is from the home taping sessions once more, it could be Leon Redbone singing it is so unlike the Nick Drake of later years. The composer is unknown but assumed to be a friend of Nick's from his college days.

STRANGE MEETING II (1967/8) was written in France and Morocco and may have been Nick's first ever song. Jackson C. Frank (an influence on Nick) had also travelled to these destinations in his 'follow the footsteps of Jack Kerouac' phase. A woman, his princess of the sand, walking along the beach together being in love for a moment and then she was gone. Like many unrequited lovers he returns to retrace his steps hoping that she just might be there. A superb lyric which was only taped onto his home machine, why it never got an album studio version remains a mystery.

RIDER ON THE WHEEL (1974), simple ordinary song the first track of the last four studio recordings. Who or what is the rider on the wheel? It could be someone on the big wheel at the funfair, or alternatively a motor-cycle rider on the wall of death, going round and round. In the earlier 'The Chime of the City Clock' Nick mentioned 'riding on the range of a London Street', so he may be on a bicycle or perhaps in a car. This lyric is a little too cryptic for me, this is yet another one for you dear reader.

BLACK EYED DOG (1974), is the track that the critics selected as announcing Nick's suicide. A country blues in the style of Robert Johnson King of the Delta Bluesmen. Sung in a wail of a voice, for the most part not recognisable as the voice of Nick Drake, the vocal is similar to Johnson or perhaps Blind Lemon Jefferson. Could this be the pirates Black Dog and Blind Pew and their dreaded 'black spot' from Robert Louis Stevenson's Treasure Island. Billy Bones had the delivery of the 'black spot', he was an old sea dog. He was always looking out for Black Dog who would one day come knocking at his door. Once the black spot had been presented it was just a matter of weeks before you died an omen of severe bad luck. Black Dog did come calling he knew Billy Bones' name, the black dog of the song knows Nick Drake's name. This is may all be extremely far fetched but it would be a portent of death. He is growing old and he wants to go home.

HANGING ON A STAR (1974), the critics acclaim his art but no-one else pays any attention. They say he is so good but just leave him there wondering. The vocal sounds as if all hope gone, resignation, all is lost.

VOICE FROM THE MOUNTAIN (1974), the last recording from February 1974. The chime returns as does the rain, a recapitulation of what has passed before. A voice is calling him from above, which seems pretty obvious, yet this voice is his friend. The last track on the last album ends with Nick Drake imploring 'Tell me with love, where can it end, voice from above'. As the sound evaporates the listener is left numb in the knowledge that no-one was there to answer the call.

103

When the album finishes the natural feeling of the listener is sadness that this is the last set of recordings that will ever be heard from such a talented singer composer. There are other poems which never achieved the luxury of a tune. Nick wrote 'Blue Season' which once again discusses nature and the elements, plus the rain of course. 'Joey in Mind' confirms that Joey is a woman. He sits waiting for her in the fog, he has only memories of her. Whilst he waits in the Saturday rain he dreams of Joey or Mary Jane. 'Outside' is agoraphobia, he is remaining inside and thinking about going outside. It is strange outside but cool inside. 'Mickey's Tune' is a dream of floating away with his lover on the breeze. If she leads he will follow, the happiness of the fairground merry-go-round, sailing the seas of forget-me-not. A lyric that would have made a beautiful song. 'Leaving Me Behind' is probably Nick feeling that he is doomed to be unsuccessful. 'Success can be gained but at too great a cost' he writes, the chances have been lost, there is a future for the wind and the rain, but Nick is being left behind.

For a short time before his death Nick lived with John and Sheila Wood. Sheila commented on Nick's long contemplative silences. In conversation she would learn from Nick just how unhappy he was. For some unknown reason she even mooted the question " If you are so unhappy Nick why haven't you killed yourself?". Nick's response was "It is too cowardly and I don't have the courage'. Nick was always embarrassed over his dependence on pills, often he would make an excuse to leave the room so that he could take them in private. Few ladies seem to have been part of his life, a girl friend Sophia Ryde confirmed the sadness Nick felt on his necessity to take pills to control his mood depressions. Daisy Burlison-Rush was another lady who spent time with Nick, she did what she could to stop Nick becoming detached from reality. In his last months Nick was saying that he felt he couldn't cope, his defence was gone.

Joe Boyd continued to work in the music industry working with Michael Stipe and R.E.M., Billy Bragg, 10,000 Maniacs, and others. A singer songwriter named Scott Appel has performed an in depth study of all Nick's guitar tunings, he even added a melody to a couple of poems supplied by Rodney and Molly Drake. This macabre curiosity by Scott Appel in Nick's work compares with the multitude of artists who tried to do the same for Jimi Hendrix and his guitar style. Appel says that Nick when guitaring used 'flesh and fingernail' on some songs and 'only fingernail' on others. He continues to say that Nick never used a 'pick' (plectrum) of any kind. There will always be impersonators but Appel does seem to be deeply immersed in Nick's work when he could be a success in his own right, he is an extremely accomplished musician. Many of the tracks on his albums would be categorised as 'New Age Music', however Scott Appel does give some beautifully caring renditions of some of Nick's songs. If you would wish to search out his second album which includes the Nick Drake poem set to music it is called 'Nine of Swords', released on School Kids Records, and Kicking Mule Records, it is unlikely that you will be disappointed.

Imaginary Records released 'BRITTLE DAYS' an album of Nick's songs sung by various artists. RIVERMAN (The Changelings) is given an Indian sound, with tablas and electronic phased sitar effects. The female vocal is extremely similar to that of Julee Cruise when singing her tracks for the soundtrack of 'Twin Peaks'. AT THE CHIME OF A CITY CLOCK (The High Llamas) has a superb bass beat, most reviewers hated this version but I think it has plenty to commend it. Sounding at times like Crowded House this is electric soft rock, and is certainly different to the original.

PINK MOON (Loop) two acoustic guitars one of which is playing the piano over-dub from Nick's original. ROAD (No Man) has the feel of Donovan accompanied by bongo drums, there is some excellent electric keyboard playing. The recording of the bongo sound which is usually is quite difficult, makes them sound like biscuit tins, or are they buscuit tins? CELLO SONG (The Walkabouts) has a great drum beat which transforms the song into a march. The female vocalist gives the version and olde folk song edge.

JOEY (Shellyann Orphan) a gentle version with Nick's piano arrangement moved to guitar. Caroline Crawley on vocal has followed all Nick's vocal mannerisms perfectly, a superb version. FROM THE MORNING (Scott Appel) the first of two songs included on this album by Scott. He has added a great guitar 'thump' with plenty of reverb to accentuate the beat. FRUIT TREE (The Times) is startling and unusual. The descending chords accompany more ethereal 'Julee Cruise' type sounds.

KNOW (Martyn Bates) is awful, pugilistic vocals, a cappella designed to infuriate, they succeed. VOICE FROM THE MOUNTAIN (The Swinging Swine) is Japanese influenced, or Jean Michel Jarre perhaps. The female voice is pure and the synthesized strings are beautifully arranged, this should have been released as a single. TIME HAS TOLD ME (Nikki Sudden and the French Revolution), is given the Sun Records rockabilly treatment. It is intentionally amateurish, Sudden has gone out of his way to make sure that his version is different. He succeeds with that but it is far too long even though he dispenses with half of Nick's lyrics.

FLY (Tracy Santa) has a problem with a muffled drum sound, the song sounds like a remaindered Neil Young out-take, Tracy is a male. NORTHERN SKY (Clive Gregson) sounds like Elton John, especially on piano, I always thought that John Cale added little to the original but this version is far worse. HAZEY JANE I (Scott Appel) a respectful reading of the song, at times Scott sings like Tim Hardin. Scott certainly has mastered Nick's guitar style perfectly. RIVERMAN (R.Stevie Moore) is the only song given two versions. They are set like bookends at the start and end of the album. I really like this version for two reasons, the first is the Moore gives the impression of being depressed and tired, and secondly this is what Nick would have sounded like still singing this song at his fortieth year in show business extravaganza. Many of the tracks are ordinary but as a complete entity the album succeeds and is enjoyable.

John Martyn had been a close friend and confidant throughout Nick's years in the public eye. It is common knowledge that they once parted in animosity due to Nick's feelings that John was selling out to the commercial-devil. The separation hurt both Nick and John, and later John wrote the song 'Solid Air' for his friend. Nick Clews of the group Dream Academy wrote 'Life in a Northern Town' and dedicated it to the memory of Nick in 1979.

There were no recriminations, the world is packed full of 'If Only' people. Nick Drake seems to have existed without any egotistical tendencies, he was 'born (in the words of sister Gabrielle) with one skin too few'.

Nick Drake stepped nervously into the spotlight for a short while and then it went out. Everyone who knew him remembers him with deep fondness, sadly I was never allowed the luxury of meeting the man, but I do have his music in my head.

'When you deem me so high, and you hear me so clear,
Why do you leave me hanging on a star'
Nick Drake (1948-1974)

KEN BROOKS 97

ACKNOWLEDGEMENTS

Jason Creed for his assistance in all things. His magazine PINK MOON is essential reading. He can be contacted at 34 Kingsbridge Road, Walton on Thames, Surrey, KT12 2BZ

Tony Coleman, Harry Allen, Michael Edwards, David Housden, Ken Brooks.

BOOKS IN THE AGENDA LISTENER'S COMPANION SERIES

AVAILABLE NOW FROM YOUR LOCAL BOOKSHOP
at £5.99 each

BUTTERFLY, THE MUSIC OF SCOTT WALKER
ISBN 1 899882 45 6
BOB DYLAN BLOTTING PAPER MAN
ISBN 1 899882 10-3
BOB DYLAN MAN IN THE LONG BLACK COAT
ISBN 1 899882 15-4
FAST AND BULBOUS THE CAPTAIN BEEFHEART STORY
ISBN 1 899882 25-1
A STRICTLY GENTEEL GENIUS THE FRANK ZAPPA STORY
PART ONE ISBN 1 899882 30-8
A STRICTLY GENTEEL GENIUS THE FRANK ZAPPA STORY
PART TWO ISBN 1 899882 35-9
VAN MORRISON, INTO THE SUNSET
ISBN 1 899882 40-5
LEONARD COHEN, CAME SO FAR FOR LOVE
ISBN 1 899882 50 2

ART BEAT READER MAGAZINE
Track-by-track reviews on many artists such as Al Kooper, Country Joe McDonald, Gordon Lightfoot, Clifford T.Ward, Boz Scaggs, Steve Miller etc, plus articles concerning the best in literature and music.
(Quarterly at £2.00 per issue)

If you have difficulty in obtaining any of the above listed books please write direct to...Agenda limited, Units 8/9 Kenyon's Trading Estate, Weyhill Road, Andover, Hampshire, U.K. SP10 3NP

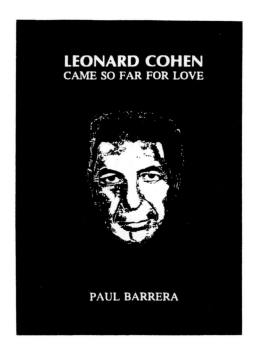

LEONARD COHEN, CAME SO FAR FOR LOVE, is a review of the songs, poetry and novels of Leonard Cohen. Leonard's work stands high in comparison to any 20th Century poet. Nearly all singer songwriters became writers second, Leonard was an acknowledged and revered poet years before he started to write songs. He changed direction when he learned that writing poetry would not pay his bills. A man of deep and creative inner strength which is evident in his work. Leonard has not produced as many albums as others but his has always maintained an extremely high standard where others have spread their intellect thinly. A track-by track listeners companion which stretches to poem-by-poem evaluations destined to have you returning to re-listen to Leonard Cohen's work anew.

LEONARD COHEN, CAME SO FAR FOR LOVE ISBN 1 899882 50 2
paperback 210 x 150mm £ 5.99

Agenda Ltd, Units 8/9 Kenyon's Trading Estate,
Weyhill Road, Andover, Hampshire, England, SP10 3NP

CURRENT TITLE

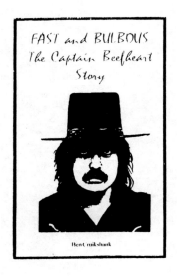

FAST AND BULBOUS THE CAPTAIN BEEFHEART STORY, *the enduring story of an innovator, and artist in oils, a sculptor in soap, and a creative poet and musician. Don van Vliet changed his name to Captain Beefheart, and transformed The Blues into his own brand of modern music. His turned his back on his success as a musician and reverted to his work as a painter, and once more received accolades from intellectuals for his new career. The story with a track-by-track analysis of his work of a man now suffering poor health who finally achieved the success he always deserved.*

CAPTAIN BEEFHEART, FAST AND BULBOUS ISBN 1 899882 25 1
paperback 210 x 150mm PRICE £ 5.99

**Agenda Ltd, Units 8/9 Kenyon's Trading Estate,
Weyhill Road, Andover, Hampshire, England, SP10 3NP**